SPIRIT OF ST. GERTRUDE;

OR,

THE LOVE OF THE HEART OF JESUS TO HIS CREATURES.

BY

THE AUTHOR OF "ST. FRANCIS AND THE FRANCISCANS,"
"THE LIFE AND REVELATIONS OF ST. GERTRUDE,"
"ST. CLARE AND THE POOR CLARES," ETC.

PREFACE.

It has been well said, that " the most ancient special devotion of Christians is that of the Sacred Heart of Jesus;" for it is simply saying that Jesus has been loved by Christians from the beginning with a love proportioned to their sanctity.   St. Augustine was the great promoter of this devotion in the early ages of the Church; St. Francis of Assisi may be said to have been its living exemplar in the ages of Faith; while the Revelations of St. Gertrude were a rich mine from whence souls drew treasures of love, and learned how the Heart of Love rewards the fidelity of His spouses.

The extracts from the Revelations of St. Gertrude contained in this little volume, have been compiled with special reference to the Devotion of the Sacred Heart. It is hoped that thus some of the most generally interesting revelations of the Saint will be made known to those who could not afford a larger and more expensive work. May these little sparks from the great furnace of the Heart of Love, inflame the souls of thousands!

The Little Office of St. Gertrude is published for the first time in English. The original, from which we have translated it, may be found in the Officium Monasticum Beatæ Mariæ Virginis, &c., Pauli V. Pont. Max. auctoritate recognitum pro omnibus sub regula S. P. Benedicti militantibus Venetiis. Ex typographia Bulleonianâ MDCCLVI.

PREFACE.

We hope, in the second edition of the Life and Revelations of St. Gertrude, to be able to give correct information about her relics—a subject on which, hitherto, much misapprehension has prevailed. We shall also be able to give interesting details of works in German, Spanish, &c., in the British Museum.

CONVENT OF POOR CLARES,
  KENMARE.
May 6, Feast of St. John before the Latin Gate.

CONTENTS.

PART I.

CONTENTS.

CONTENTS.

PART II.

PART III.

CONTENTS.

PART IV

THE LOVE OF THE HEART OF JESUS TOWARDS THE SOULS IN PURGATORY.

CONTENTS.

PART V

REVELATIONS OF THE LOVE OF THE HEART OF JESUS TO HIS MOTHER.

CONTENTS.

THE

SPIRIT OF ST. GERTRUDE.

PART I.

Revelations of the Love of the Heart of Jesus to His Creatures.

CHAPTER I.

OUR dear Lord has not forbidden the mutual love of His creatures; on the contrary, He has sanctified and ennobled it by His own example and by the example of His saints. It is only when we give to the creature what of right belongs alone to the Creator, that He complains. Thus we find an example of hallowed affection for a creature, in the singular love which all who knew Gertrude felt for her, and in the special love of the dear, though unknown friend, to whom we owe the careful compilation of her revelations.

It was revealed on one occasion to a person of great sanctity, as she prayed for Gertrude, why the Saint was so singularly dear to the Sacred Heart. " O Divine Love," she exclaimed, " what is it You behold in this virgin which obliges You to esteem her so highly and to love her so much ?" Our Lord replied : " It is My goodness alone which obliges Me ; since she contains and perfects in her soul those five virtues which please Me above all others, and which I have placed therein by a singular liberality. She possesses purity, by a continual influence of My grace ; she possesses humility, amidst the great diversity of gifts which I have bestowed on her—for the more I effect in her, the more she abases herself ; she possesses a true benignity, which makes her desire the salvation of the whole world for My greater glory ; she possesses a true fidelity, spreading abroad, without reserve, all her treasures for the same end. Finally, she possesses a consummate charity ; for she loves Me with her whole heart, with her whole soul, and with her whole strength ; and for love of Me, she loves her neighbour as herself."

After our Lord had spoken thus to this soul, He showed her a precious stone on His heart, in the form of a triangle, made of trefoils, the beauty and brilliancy of which cannot be described; and He said to her: "I always wear this jewel as a pledge of the affection which I have for My spouse. I have made it in this form, that all the celestial court may know by the brightness of the first leaf that there is no creature on earth so dear to Me as Gertrude, because there is no one at this present time amongst mankind who is united to Me so closely as she is, either by purity of intention or by uprightness of will. They will see by the second leaf, that there is no soul still bound by the chains of flesh and blood whom I am so disposed to enrich by My graces and favours. And they will observe in the splendour of the third leaf, that there is no one who refers to My glory alone the gifts received from Me with such sincerity and fidelity as Gertrude; who, far from wishing to claim the least thing for herself, desires most ardently that nothing shall be ever attributed to her." Our Lord concluded the revelation thus: "You cannot find Me in any place in which I delight more, or which is more suitable for Me, than in the Sacrament of the Altar, and after that, in the heart and soul of Gertrude, My beloved; for towards her all My affections, and the complacences of My divine love, turn in a singular manner."*

On another occasion, a devout person, who was praying for the Saint, heard these words : "She for whom thou prayest is My dove, who has no guile in her, for she rejects from her heart as gall all the guile and bitterness of sin. She is My chosen lily, which I love to bear in My hands ; for it is My delight and My pleasure to repose in the purity and innocence of this chaste soul. She is My rose, whose odour is full of sweetness, because of her patience in every adversity, and the thanksgivings which she continually offers Me, which ascend before Me as the sweetest perfumes. She is that spring flower which never fades, and which I take pleasure in contemplating, because she keeps and maintains continually in her breast an ardent desire not only for all virtues, but for the utmost perfection of every virtue. She is as a sweet melody, which ravishes the ears of the blessed ; and this melody is composed of all the sufferings she endures with so much constancy."

* It is generally supposed, but without sufficient authority, that these words were addressed to St. Mechtilde. She *may* have been the "holy person" to whom the revelation was made; but this opinion is merely conjectural.

CHAPTER II.

HOW THE HEART OF JESUS LOVES AND REWARDS OUR CONFIDENCE.

THE Saint's confidence in God was indeed an eminent characteristic of her sanctity, and one which obtained for her immense favours. How could the Heart of Jesus refuse anything to one who trusted Him so entirely? How pleasing this virtue was to her Spouse was revealed to one of her religious, who had long prayed in vain for a particular favour, which she ardently desired. At last our Divine Lord vouchsafed to inform her of the reason of this delay, at which she had felt and expressed her profound amazement. "I have delayed answering your prayers, because you have not yet sufficient confidence in the effects which My mercy produces in you. Why do you not act like Gertrude, My chosen virgin, who is so firmly established on My Providence, that there is nothing which she does not hope for from the plenitude of My grace; therefore I will never refuse her anything, whatever she may ask Me."

A holy man once earnestly prayed that he might know what virtue was most pleasing to our Lord in His spouse. He was answered, that it was " her generosity of heart."* But as this surprised him not a little, he ventured to reply: " As for me, O Lord, I had imagined that what pleased You most in this soul was the perfect knowledge she had of herself, and the high degree of love to which, by Your grace, she has attained." Our Lord replied : " This generosity of heart is of such value and so great a good, that the height of perfection may be obtained through it. By means of it My elect is prepared at all times for receiving gifts of great value, which prevents her from attaching her heart to anything which could either impede Me or displease Me."

It was the custom of the Saint, when she was offered any choice in articles of clothing or other necessaries, to close her eyes, and then to put out her hand and take whatever she touched. Then she received whatever fell to her lot with the most lively gratitude, as a present from our Lord Himself. Indeed, her devotion to Divine Pro-

* " Respondit Dominus : Libertas cordis ;" but the word "freedom" or "generosity" seems to give the idea more correctly in English.

vidence was a special feature in her sanctity, and one which procured her many favours. What could be refused to one who trusted so utterly to Eternal Love!

Hence this soul became so united to Jesus as to have no will but His, so that our Divine Jesus Himself said to St. Mechtilde: "I have united My Heart so closely to her soul by the ties of My mercy, that she has become one spirit with Me. It is on this account she obeys so promptly all the desires of My will; so that the harmony and understanding which exists between the different members of the body and the heart is not greater than that which exists between the soul of Gertrude and Mine; and as the moment a man has willed in his heart a movement of his hands, they accomplish his desire, because they are entirely subject to the will of the heart; and as one desires in his mind that his eyes should look on any object, and his eyes immediately open to obey him,—so Gertrude is ever with Me, and at every moment is ready to obey the movements which I suggest."

A similar revelation was made about the same time to another holy person, to whom it was said, that the union of the Saint with her Spouse would become even yet more perfect, that she would receive the gifts of God with yet greater abundance, and that she would attain so perfect a union with Him, that with her eyes she would only see what God willed her to see, with her ears only hear what He willed her to hear, and with her lips only speak what He willed her to speak.

That one so united to God should have been specially favoured with the gift of miracles, is but what we might expect in the ordinary course of spiritual life. Those who give themselves up without reserve to God, receive His gifts also without reserve. They do His will, and He accomplishes theirs: for the will of the Bridegroom and the bride is one. The Saint once obtained the cessation of a frost, which was so severe, that had it continued longer the fruits of the earth would have been utterly destroyed. Her petition was offered at the Holy Sacrifice ; and as she was about to approach the adorable Sacrament of the Altar, our Lord assured her that He had granted her request. With holy boldness, however, she asked that the hail which was then falling might instantly cease. Her petition was granted ; but as she was absorbed in the greatness of the action she was about to perform, she thought no more of her request.

It was only remembered as she left the church, and saw the thaw which had already commenced. Those who knew not of the prayer of the Saint were greatly amazed at the sudden change of weather, and feared it was but a passing cessation of the dreaded severity; but it was not so: the country was spared desolation and famine, though few knew to whom they were indebted for this favour.

It was the Saint's ordinary custom to have recourse to her heavenly Spouse in every trial, whether of less or greater import; and her prayers were equally accepted on all such occasions. What, indeed, is little in His sight, who so cares for His elect, that the very hairs of their head are numbered, and not one can fall without His knowledge? Thus it is related of Gertrude, that even when she had lost a needle with which she had been working, and had sought it for some time in the straw where it had fallen, she turned to her Lord, for whose glory it had been used, and asked Him to help her in her search; even as she spoke, she put her hand once more into the straw, and found instantly what she had so long looked for in vain. Indeed, so great was the power of the Saint over the Heart of her Spouse, that it appeared as if

our Divine Lord Himself was pained to refuse
her any request.   It happened on one occasion,
that a long continuance of drought, combined
with tempestuous weather, caused serious fears
for the fruits of the earth.   St. Gertrude, as
usual, had recourse to prayer.   It was not the
will of God to grant her petition; but, with
amazing condescension, He vouchsafed not only
to inform her of His designs, but even, as it
would appear, to excuse Himself to her for not
complying with her request.

"The reason which obliges Me sometimes to
grant the prayers of My elect, does not exist between you and Me; since our wills are so closely
united by the sacred tie of grace, that you desire
nothing but what I Myself desire.   But because
I design by the terrors of this tempest to conquer some who rebel against My will, and at
least to oblige them to seek Me by prayer, since
they only come to Me when they have no other
resource, it is necessary that I should refuse you
what you desire.   Nevertheless, that you may
know that your prayers have not failed in their
effect,. I will grant you in return some other
spiritual favour."

CHAPTER IV.

HOW THE HEART OF JESUS LOVES AND
REWARDS CONFORMITY TO HIS WILL IN
SICKNESS.

DURING the last illness of the Saint, as
the religious, who were so singularly devoted to her, prayed for her with great
fervour, our Lord replied to her : "I have waited
with inexpressible joy for this moment, that I
might lead My elect into solitude, and there
speak to her heart. I have not been disap-
pointed in My expectation, for she conforms
herself in all things to My will, and obeys Me
in the manner which is most agreeable to Me."
The holy Benedictine understood that by solitude
our Lord meant the illness of the Saint, in
which He spoke to the heart of His beloved,
and not to her ear ; for His language is such as
cannot be understood in an ordinary manner,
just as those things which are spoken to the
heart are rather felt than heard. Tribulations
and afflictions of heart are the Lord's language
to His elect ; when one who suffers thus reflects
that they are useless, that they are spending

their time uselessly—that others are labouring for them, and labouring in vain, inasmuch as they are never to recover their health through this labour—the soul answers to such thoughts, that what is most pleasing to God is to maintain interior patience, and to desire that the entire will of God may be accomplished in them. Such an answer does not reach heaven in the usual manner of human communications, but resounds, as it were, through that sweetest Divine organ, the Heart of Jesus, which is the ecstatic joy of the entire Trinity and the heavenly host. He continued thus : "My beloved affords Me the most intense and agreeable delight, because she despises not the afflictions of infirmity, as Queen Vasthi despised the orders of King Assuerus, when he commanded her to appear with a diadem on her head, that she might exhibit her beauty to his nobles. So, when I take pleasure in displaying the beauty of My chosen one in the presence of the ever-adorable Trinity and the heavenly host, I oppress her with sickness and infirmity; and she carries out my intentions to My perfect satisfaction, when, with all patience, she the more willingly and discreetly receives the relief and comfort I choose to give her body ; and it adds to her glory that she sometimes does this with inconvenience to herself: but it should be her consolation to recollect that all things work together unto good to those that love God." (Rom. viii.)

On another occasion, while the same religious was praying for her, the Lord said to her : "It is a pleasure to Me to have My chosen one prepare a lodging for Me, and then to bestow on her pearls and flowers of gold. By pearls I mean her senses, by flowers of gold her leisure, with which, when she has time, and her strength is somewhat restored, she discharges her duty as well as she can, in preparing most becoming and acceptable ornaments for Me; being solicitous how she may so arrange everything that can tend to increase and preserve religion, so that after her death her rules and example may be as a firm pillar to support religion in eternal praise. But in the height of her labours, if she feels that she is injuring her health, she immediately desists, and leaves Me to finish the work ; for the real fidelity that moves My Heart consists in persons discharging their duty when they find themselves in good health, and immediately desisting and intrusting all to me when they find themselves indisposed."

As the illness of the Saint increased, she be-

came incapable of the least manual labour, and
her tender conscience was filled with fear lest
there should be any imperfection even in this
compulsory inactivity; she therefore requested
the religious who had received so many revelations for her consolation to pray for her.   Our
Lord replied :

"A good king never takes it ill of his queen
if she neglect bringing forward at a given hour
the ornaments that he is most gratified at receiving; but is much more pleased at finding
her always ready to comply with his wishes :
and the sweetness of My most benign Heart
delights more in the patient endurance with
which My chosen one bears her infirmity, on
the relief of which she resumes her labours for
the extension of religion, so far as she can do
so without injuring her health."

As the Saint found herself daily more and
more unequal to the important duties of her
office, she became anxious to resign her charge ;
but even this desire she was unwilling to put
into effect, until assured that it was the will of
God.   Fearful lest her own inclination might de-
ceive her, even in the interpretation of heavenly
communications, she requested her favoured
daughter to ask the counsel she needed from the

Source of all wisdom. Our Lord condescended to reply—may we not hope for the consolation and help of many of His chosen ones, as well as of the soul so singularly favoured thus specially to know His will?—"By this illness I sanctify My chosen one, to make her a fit habitation for Myself—as a church is sanctified by the blessing of a bishop. In like manner as a church is secured with locks, to prevent the entrance of the unworthy, so I, by this infirmity, seal her up so that her mind cannot be occupied by externals, which tend to disturb the heart and distract it from Me."

CHAPTER V.

HOW THE HEART OF JESUS REWARDS DEVOTION TO HIS PASSION.

ONE night a crucifix, which the Saint had near her bed, seemed to bow down towards her, and she exclaimed: "O my sweet Jesus, why dost Thou thus abase Thyself?" He replied: "The love of My Divine Heart attracts Me to you." Then she took the image and placed it on her heart, caressing it tenderly, and saying: "A bundle of myrrh is my Beloved to me" (Cant. i.); to which our Lord replied, interrupting her: "I will carry Him in my bosom;" making her to understand by this that we ought to hide in His adorable Passion all the pains we suffer, whether of body or mind, as we would place a prop* in a bundle of sticks. Thus those who are tempted to impatience by adversity, should recall to mind the adorable patience of the Son of God, who was led like a meek lamb to the slaughter for our salvation, and never opened His mouth to utter the least word of impatience. And when any one is disposed to revenge the ill that has been done to him, either in word or deed, he should endeavour to recall to himself with what peace of heart his Beloved Jesus suffered, not rendering evil for evil, nor testifying the least resentment by His words; but, on the contrary, rewarding those who made Him suffer, by redeeming them by His sufferings and His death: and thus let us endeavour, according to the example of our Lord, to do good for evil. So also, if any one entertains a mortal hatred towards those who have offended him, he ought to remember the exceeding sweetness with which the Son of God prayed for His

* "Sudem."

executioners, even when enduring the very torments of His Passion, and in the agony of death praying for His crucifiers with these words: "Father, forgive them," &c. (Luke, xxiii.); and, in union with this love, let us pray for our enemies. Our Lord then said: "Whosoever hides his sufferings and adversities in the bouquet of My Passion, and joins them on to such of My sufferings as they seem most to resemble, he truly reposes in My bosom, and I will give him, to augment his merits, all that My singular charity has merited by My patience and by My other virtues."

The Saint inquired : " How, O Lord, do You receive the special devotion which some have for the image of Your cross?" Our Lord replied : "It is very acceptable to me; nevertheless, when those who have a special devotion to these representations of My cross fail to imitate the example of My Passion, their conduct is like that of a mother, who, to gratify herself and for her own honour, adorns her daughter with different ornaments, but refuses her harshly what she most desires to have. While this mother deprives her child of what she wishes for, the child cares little for all else that is given to her, because she knows it is done through pride, and not from affection. So all the testimonies of love, respect, and reverence which are offered to the image of My cross, will not be perfectly acceptable to Me unless the examples of My Passion are also imitated."

One Friday, when the Saint had spent the whole night in meditation, and had been prevented from sleeping by the ardour of her love, she remembered with what tenderness she had snatched the iron nails from a crucifix which she always kept near her, and replaced them by nails of sweet-smelling cloves, and she said to God : "My Beloved, how didst Thou accept my drawing the iron nails from the sacred Wounds of Thy Hands and Feet, to place these cloves therein, which give an agreeable odour?" Our Lord replied : " It was so agreeable to Me, that in return for it I poured forth the noble balsam of My Divinity into the wounds of your sins. And for this all the saints will praise Me eternally; for your wounds, by the infusion of this liquor, will become agreeable." " But, Lord," inquired the Saint, "wilt Thou not grant the same grace to those who perform the same action?" "Not to all," He replied ; " but those who do it with the same fervour will receive a similar reward ; and those who, following your example, do likewise, with all the devotion of which they are capable, will receive a lesser recompense."

Gertrude then took the crucifix and clasped it in her arms, kissing it tenderly, until she felt herself growing weak from her long vigil, when she laid it aside, and taking leave of her Spouse,* asked His permission to go and rest, that she might recover her strength, which was almost exhausted by her long meditation. After she had spoken thus, she turned from the crucifix and composed herself to sleep. But as she reposed, our Lord stretched forth His right Hand from the cross to embrace her, and whispered these words to her : " Listen to Me, My beloved; I will sing you a canticle of love." And then He commenced, in a tender and harmonious voice, to sing the following verse to the chant of the hymn *Rex Christe, factor omnium :*

> " Amor meus continuus
> Tibi languor assiduus :
> Amor tuus suavissimus
> Mihi sapor gratissimus."†

Having finished the verse, He said : " Now, My

---

* "Vale dilecte mi, et habe bonam noctem."

† The hymn *Rex Christe* may be found in Gerbert's *Monumenta veteris Liturgiæ Alemannicæ.* It was com-

beloved, instead of the *Kyrie eleison*, which is sung at the end of each verse of the hymn *Rex Christe*, ask what you will, and I will grant it to you." The Saint then prayed for some particular intentions, and her prayers were favourably heard. Our Lord again chanted the same verse, and at the end again exhorted Gertrude to pray. This He repeated many times, at different intervals, not allowing her a moment's rest, until she became completely exhausted. She then slept a little before daybreak; but the Lord Jesus, who is always near those who love Him, appeared to her in her sleep. He seemed to prepare a delicious feast for her in the Sacred Wound of His adorable Side, and He Himself placed the food in her mouth in order to refresh her; so that when she awoke she found that she had been marvellously strengthened during her sleep, for which she returned most humble and ardent thanks to God.

posed by St. Gregory the Great, and was formerly chanted at Tenebræ after the *Benedictus*. The verse to this chant is extremely difficult to render in English:

"The more I love thee, yet the more
Thou seek'st this burning fire;
While thy dear love is still to me
Sweetness I still desire."

CHAPTER VI.

HOW THE HEART OF JESUS REWARDS AND TREASURES OUR SUFFERINGS.

AS Gertrude offered to God in her prayers all that she suffered in body and mind, and all the pleasures of which she had deprived herself, whether in the flesh or the spirit, our Lord appeared to her, and showed her the pleasures and the pains which she had offered to Him under the form of two rings, enriched with precious stones, which He wore to adorn His hands. The Saint, perceiving this, repeated the offering frequently; and when suffering a corporal affliction some time afterwards, she beheld Jesus her Lord touch her left eye with the ring which He carried in His left hand, and which represented corporal afflictions and sufferings; and from this moment she felt extreme suffering in this eye, which she had beheld our Lord touch in spirit, and this pain was never entirely removed.

She knew from this, that as the ring is the sign of espousal, so also sufferings in body or mind are testimonies of the spiritual espousal of

the soul with God ; so that whoever suffers may
say confidently, with all truth : " My Lord Jesus
Christ has espoused me to Him with His ring ;"
and if he recognises in those afflictions the
graces which he has received, and returns thanks,
he may add : " He has adorned me with a crown
as His spouse ;" because thanksgiving in tribu-
lation is a crown of glory more brilliant than
gold, and incomparably more precious than
topaz.

On one occasion, when the Saint was prevented from assisting at Vespers, by some infirmity, she exclaimed : " Lord, wouldest Thou
not be more honoured if I were in choir with the
community, engaged in prayer, and fulfilling the
duties of my Rule, than by my being here, passing
my time uselessly, in consequence of this illness?"
Our Lord replied : " Be assured that the bridegroom takes more pleasure in conversing with
his bride familiarly in his house, than when he
displays her before the world, adorned with her
richest ornaments." By these words she understood that the soul appears in public, and
clothed with all her state, when she occupies
herself in good works for the glory of God ; but
that she reposes in secret with her Spouse, when
she is hindered by any infirmity from attending

to those exercises, for in this state she is deprived
of the satisfaction of acting according to her own
inclination, and she remains abandoned entirely
to the will of God ; and therefore it is that God
takes most pleasure in us when we find least
occasion of pleasing and glorifying ourselves.

CHAPTER VII.

HOW THE HEART OF JESUS ASSISTS OUR IMPERFECT EFFORTS.

ONCE, as the Saint was reciting the Divine
Office with extraordinary fervour, on the
Feast of a Saint, each word which she
uttered appeared to dart like an arrow from her
heart into the Heart of Jesus, penetrating it
deeply, and filling it with ineffable satisfaction.
From one end of these arrows rays of light shot
forth like stars, which seemed to fall on all the
saints, but especially on the one whose festival
was celebrated ; from the lower end of the
arrows drops of dew flowed forth, which fer-
tilized the souls of the living, and refreshed the
souls in purgatory.

As the Saint endeavoured on another occasion

to attach some particular intention to each note and each word of her chant, she was often hindered by the weakness of nature, and at last exclaimed, with much sadness : " Alas ! what fruit can I obtain from this exercise, when I am so unstable ?" But our Lord, who could not endure to behold the affliction of His servant, with His own hands presented her with His Divine Heart, under the figure of a burning lamp, saying to her : " Behold, I present to the eyes of your soul My loving Heart, which is the organ of the most Holy Trinity, that it may accomplish all that you cannot accomplish yourself, and thus all will seem perfect in you to My eyes ; for even as a faithful servant is always ready to execute the commands of his master, so, from henceforth, my Heart will be always ready, at any moment, to repair your defects and negligences."

Gertrude wondered and feared, because of this amazing goodness of her Lord, thinking that it was not becoming for the adorable Heart, which is the treasure-house* of the Divinity, and the fruitful source of every good, to remain continually near so miserable a creature, to supply

* Gazophylacium.

for her defects, even as a servant attends on his master. But the Lord consoled and encouraged her by this comparison : " If you have a beautiful and melodious voice, and take much pleasure in chanting, will you not feel displeased if another person, whose voice is harsh and unpleasant, and who can scarcely utter a correct sound, wishes to sing instead of you, and insists on doing so ? Thus My Divine Heart, understanding human inconstancy and frailty, desires with incredible ardour continually to be invited, either by your words, or at least by some other sign, to operate and accomplish in you what you are not able to accomplish yourself; and as its omnipotence enables it to act without trouble, and its impenetrable wisdom enables it to act in the most perfect manner, so also its joyous and loving charity makes it ardently desire to accomplish this end."

CHAPTER VIII.

OF THE ABUNDANT VIRTUE WHICH FLOWS FROM THE HEART OF JESUS INTO THE FAITHFUL SOUL.

SOME days after, as the Saint reflected upon this stupendous favour with singular gratitude, she anxiously inquired of the Lord how long it would be continued to her. He replied : "As long as you desire to have it; for it would grieve Me to deprive you of it." She answered : " But is it possible that Thy Deified Heart is suspended like a lamp in the midst of mine, which is, alas ! so unworthy of its presence, when at the same time I have the joy of finding in Thyself this very same source of all delight?" "It is even so," replied the Lord: "when you wish to take hold of any thing, you stretch forth your hand, and then withdraw it again after you have taken it ; so also the love which I bear towards you causes Me to extend My Heart to draw you to Me, when you are distracting yourself with exterior things ; and then, when you have recollected yourself, I withdraw My Heart, and you along with it, so that you may enter into Me; and thus I make you taste the sweetness of all virtues."

Then, as she considered on the one hand, with exceeding wonder and gratitude, the greatness of the charity which God had for her, and, on the other, her own nothingness and the great number of her faults, she retired with profound self-contempt into the valley of humility, esteeming herself unworthy of any grace; and having remained therein hidden for some time, He who loves to pour forth His gifts on the humble, seemed to make a golden tube* come forth from His Heart, which descended upon this humble soul in the form of a lamp, making a channel through which He poured forth on her the abundance of all His graces; so that when she humbled herself at the recollection of her faults, our Lord poured forth on her from His sacred Heart all the virtue and beauty of His Divine perfection, which concealed her imperfections from the eyes of the Divine Goodness. And further, if she desired any new ornament, or any of those things which appeared attractive and desirable to the human heart, it was com-

* Fistulam.

municated to her, with much pleasure and joy, by this same mysterious canal.

When she had tasted the sweetness of these holy delights for some time, and was adorned with all virtues—not her own, but those given her by God—she heard a most melodious sound, as of a sweet harper harping upon his harp, and these words were sung to her: "Come, O Mine own, to Me: enter, O Mine own, into Me: abide, O Mine own, with me."* And the Lord Himself explained the meaning of this canticle to her, saying: "Come to Me, because I love you, and desire that you should be always present before Me, as My beloved spouse, and therefore I call you; and because My delights are in you, I desire that you should enter into Me. Furthermore, because I am the God of love, I desire that you should remain indissolubly united to Me, even as the body is united to the spirit, without which it cannot live for a moment." This rapture continued for an hour, and the Saint was drawn in a miraculous manner into the Heart of

---

* "Audivit quandam vocem dulcissimam, tanquam cytharistæ suaviter demulcenti melodiâ cytharizantis in cythara sua, hæc verba. Veni mea ad me : Intra meum in me : Mane meus mecum." Had she, then, indeed heard that ineffable song which will be the joy and the eternal consolation of the redeemed ?

Jesus, through this sacred channel of which we have spoken, so that she found herself happily reposing in the Bosom of her Lord and Spouse. What she felt, what she saw, what she heard, what she tasted, what she learned of the words of life, she alone can know, and they who, like her, are worthy to be admitted to this sublime union with their Spouse Jesus, their soul's true love, who is God, blessed for ever. Amen.

CHAPTER IX..

HOW THE SOUL MAY SEEK GOD, AND TRANS-FIGURE ITSELF INTO HIM, IN FOUR WAYS.

WHILE the Antiphon, *In lectulo meo*,* was chanted, in which the words *quem diligit anima mea* are repeated four times, she reflected on four different manners in which the faithful soul may seek God.

By the first words, "By night I sought Him whom my soul loveth," she understood the first

---

* "In my bed, by night, I sought Him whom my soul loveth" (Cant. iii. 1); commencement of i. Lesson, i. Nocturn, Feast of St. Mary Magdalen, but not used now as an Antiphon.

way of seeking God, by the praises and blessings which are offered to Him on the sacred couch of contemplation. Hence the words, "I sought Him, and found Him not," follow immediately; because while the soul is imprisoned in the flesh she cannot praise God perfectly.

She understood the second manner of seeking God in the words, "I will rise, and will go about the city: in the streets and the broad ways I will seek Him whom my soul loveth;" because the various thanksgivings which the soul renders to God for all the gifts with which He enriches His creatures, are expressed by the words "the streets and broad ways." And as we cannot praise God in this world as He should be praised for all His gifts, the words, "I sought Him, and I found Him not," are added.

By these words, "The watchman found me," she understood the justice and mercy of God, which cause the soul to enter into herself, and then to compare her unworthiness with the benefits which she has received from God; so that she begins by her grief and repentance for her faults to seek His mercy, saying: "Have you seen Him whom my soul loveth?" And thus, as she has no faith in her own merits, she turns with humble confidence to the Divine mercy, and by the fervour of her prayers, and the inspiration of grace, she at last finds Him whom the faithful soul seeks.

This Antiphon being concluded, she felt her heart deeply moved by all the sweetness with which the Divine mercy had filled it during this time, and with many other graces which it would be impossible to describe, so that even her bodily strength failed her. Then she said to God : " It seems to me that I can truly say to Thee now, ' Behold, my beloved Lord ! not only my inmost soul, but every part of my body, is moved towards Thee !' " " I know and feel it perfectly," replied our Lord, " because these graces have flowed from Me and returned to Me. But as for you, who are held captive in the chains of mortality, you can never understand all the reciprocal sweetness which My Divinity feels towards you." He added: "Know, however, that this movement of grace glorifies you, as My Body was glorified on Mount Thabor, in presence of My three beloved disciples ; so that 1 can say of you, in the sweetness of My charity: ' This is my beloved daughter, in whom I am well pleased.' For it is the property of this grace to communicate to the body as well as to the mind a marvellous glory and brightness."

CHAPTER X.

OF A MYSTIC TUBE BY WHICH WE MAY DRAW
EVERY GRÁCE FROM THE HEART OF JESUS.

AT the Mass *Veni et ostende*,* the Lord appeared to St. Gertrude, full of sweetness and grace, breathing forth a holy
vivifying odour, and pouring forth from the
august throne of His glory the influences of His
love for the sweet Feast of His Nativity.

Then, the Saint having prayed Him to enrich
all who had been recommended to her prayers
with special grace, He said to her : " I have given
to each a tube of pure gold ; of which such is
the virtue, that by it they may draw forth all
they need from my Sacred Heart." By this
mystic tube she understood that good will by
which men may acquire all the spiritual riches
which are in heaven and on earth. For example:
if any one, burning with the fire of pure and holy
desires, endeavours to give God as much thanks
and praise, and as many testimonies of service

* Introit for Saturday in Ember Week ; Advent.
" Come, O Lord, and show unto us Thy face," &c.

and fidelity as certain of His saints have rendered to Him, the infinite goodness of God regards this good will as if it had really been effected. But this tube becomes more brilliant than gold when men thank God for having given them so noble and elevated a will, that they might have acquired infinitely greater advantages by it than the whole world could bestow.

She knew, also, that all her sisters who surrounded Jesus Christ received Divine grace by similar tubes. Some appeared to receive it directly from the Heart of Jesus Christ, others from His Hands; but the further from His Heart they drew these graces, the more difficulty they had in obtaining them; whereas those who drew them from His Divine Heart obtained them more easily, more sweetly, and more abundantly. Those who drew directly from His Sacred Heart represented those persons who conform themselves entirely to the Divine will, who desire above all things that this will should be accomplished in them, both in regard to spirituals and temporals. And these persons touch the Heart of God so powerfully, and render it so favourable to them at the time that God has determined, that they receive the torrent of Divine sweetness with as much abundance and pleasure as

C

e abandoned themselves perfectly to His holy will. But those who endeavoured to draw their graces from the other members of the Body of Jesus Christ, represent those persons who endeavour to acquire virtue according to their natural inclinations; and the fear and difficulty they experience is proportionate to the extent to which they have relied on their own judgment, and have failed to abandon themselves to Divine Providence.

§ 1. *Of the most perfect manner of offering our hearts to God.*

As Gertrude offered her heart to God in the following manner—" Lord, behold my heart, which is detached from all creatures; I offer it to Thee freely, beseeching Thee to purify it in the sanctifying Waters of Thy adorable Side, and to adorn it with the precious Blood of Thy sweetest Heart, and to unite it to Thee by the odours of charity "—our Lord appeared to her, and offered her heart to His Eternal Father, united to His own, under the form of a chalice, the two parts of which were joined together by wax. The Saint, perceiving this, said, with extreme fervour: " Grant me the grace, most loving Lord, that my heart may be always before Thee like the flasks* which princes use, so that Thou mayest have it cleansed and filled and emptied, according to Thy good pleasure, whenever and however Thou willest." This request being heard favourably by the Son of God, He said to His Father: "Eternal Father, may this soul pour forth for Thy infinite glory what Mine contains in My Humanity!" And from that moment, whenever the Saint offered her heart to God, saying the words above mentioned, it seemed to her so filled, that it poured itself forth in thanksgiving and praises, augmenting the joy of the blessed in heaven, and contributing to the adornment of the just on earth, as will be seen hereafter. From this moment the Saint knew that God willed her to commit to writing what He had revealed to her, that it might be for the benefit of many.

§ 2. *Of confidence in God, and of reparation for the contempts offered to Him.*

In Advent, by the response *Ecce venit*,† she

---

* "Flasconum, qui ad refectionem dominorum deferunter."

† V. Response, ii. Nocturn, 2nd Sunday in Advent: "Behold, the Lord our Protector cometh, the Holy One of Israel."

knew that if any one formed in their heart, with a firm purpose, a perfect desire of submitting in all things to the adorable will of God, alike in prosperity as in adversity, they would, by His grace, render the same honour to God by this thought as if they crowned Him with a royal diadem.

And by these words of the Prophet Isaias : " Arise, arise ! stand up, O Jerusalem !" she understood the advantage which the Church militant receives from the devotion of the elect. For when a soul, full of love, turns to God with her whole heart, and with a perfect will of repairing, were it possible, all the dishonour done to Jesus Christ, she appeases His anger by her loving charity, so that He is willing to pardon the sins of the whole world.

By the words, " That hast drunk the cup of His wrath even to the bottom" (Is. li.), may be understood how she has averted the severity of Divine justice. But by the following words, " That hast drunk even to the dregs," she knew that the reprobate have the dregs of this chalice for their portion, and can never obtain redemption.

§ 3. *Of refraining from useless words.*

By these words of Isaias, "Thou dost not thy own ways, and thy own will is not found to speak a word" (lviii. 13), she knew that he who regulates his words and actions thoughtfully, and abstains even from those that are lawful when they are not necessary, will obtain a triple advantage: first, he will find a greater pleasure in God, according to these words, "Thou shalt be delighted in the Lord;" secondly, bad thoughts will have less power over him, for it is said, "I will lift thee above the high places of the earth;" and thirdly, in eternity the Son of God will communicate the merits of His most holy life more abundantly to him than to others, because by it he has been victorious over every temptation, and gained a glorious victory, as these words express, "I will feed thee with the inheritance of Jacob thy father."

God made known to her also, by these words, "Behold, his reward is with him" (Is. xl.), that our Lord Himself, by His love, is the reward of His elect; and He insinuates Himself into their souls with such sweetness, that they may truly say they are rewarded beyond all their deserts. "And his work is before him:" that is to say, when we abandon ourselves entirely to Divine Providence, and seek only the accomplishment of the will of God in all things, grace has already rendered us perfect in the sight of God.

By the words, "Be ye holy, children of Israel," Gertrude learned that those who repent promptly of the sins they have committed, and set themselves with a sincere heart to keep the commandments of God, are as truly sanctified and as promptly cured as the leper to whom our Lord said : "I will : be thou made clean." By the words, "Sing ye to the Lord a new canticle" (Ps. cxlix.), she knew that he sings a new canticle who sings with devotion; because, when he has received the grace from God to understand what he sings, his chant becomes agreeable to God.

§ 4. *God sends afflictions to cure our souls.*

By the words, "The spirit of the Lord is upon me ; He hath sent Me to heal the contrite of heart" (Is. lxi.), she understood that the Son of God, having been sent by His Father to heal contrite hearts, was accustomed to send some affliction to His elect, even should it be only exterior, in order to heal them. But when this happens, He does not always deliver them from the affliction which has made them contrite, because it is not hurtful to them; for He prefers to cure that which might cause them eternal death.

By the words, *In splendoribus sanctorum**— " In the brightness of the saints " (Ps. cix.), she knew that the light of the Divinity is so great and so incomprehensible, that even if each saint who has lived or who will live, from the time of Adam to the end of the world, were given a special knowledge of it, as clear, as elevated, and as extended as could be given to any creature, so that none should be able to explain it to the other, nor to share in their knowledge—even should the number of saints be a thousand times greater than it is—the Divinity would still remain infinitely beyond their conception. Thus it is not written *splendore*, but *in splendoribus*— " In the brightness [plu.] of Thy saints; from the womb, before the day-star, I begot Thee."

---

* Antiphon at ii. Vespers of the Nativity, from the first Psalm at Vespers for Sundays and Festivals. These revelations were probably made during Advent, when the prophecies of Isaias are read at Matins.

CHAPTER XI.

HOW THE LOVERS OF JESUS CRUCIFIED MUST CARRY THEIR CROSS AFTER HIM.

How we must carry our cross after Jesus Christ, and how the mercy of God chastises the elect.

AT the Antiphon *Qui vult**—" If any man will come after Me, let him take up his cross and follow Me" (Matt. xvi.)—Gertrude beheld our Lord walking on a road which seemed pleasant, because of the beauty of the verdure and flowers which covered it, but which nevertheless was narrow, and rough with thorns. Then she beheld a cross which went before Him, and separated the thorns from one another, making the road wider and more easy ; while the Saviour turned to those who came after Him, and encouraged them, looking at them with a sweet and loving countenance, and saying : " Let him that will come after Me take up his cross, and deny himself, and follow Me."   By this she knew that

* Ant. at Magnificat of ii. Vespers, Com. of one Martyr.

our temptations are our crosses. For example: it is a cross to one person to be obliged by obedience to do what she dislikes; to another, to be restrained. Now, each ought so to carry his cross as to be willing to suffer with a good heart all that crosses him, and yet to neglect nothing which he thinks may be for the glory of God.

———

CHAPTER XII.

THEY WHO LABOUR FOR THE ADVANCEMENT OF RELIGION ARE REWARDED AS IF THEY HAD CLOTHED THE SAVIOUR—ANGELS ENCOMPASS THE BLEST.

BY the Response which commences *Induit me,** Gertrude learned that he who labours by his works and by his words for the advancement of religion, and the defence of justice, acts as if he clothed God Himself with a magnificent and sumptuous garment; and the Lord will recompense him in the life eternal,

* "The Lord hath clothed me," Common of Virgins, xi. Response, iii. Nocturn.

according to the riches of His royal liberality, by clothing him with a robe of gladness, and crowning him with a diadem of glory : but, above all, that he who suffers for the promotion of good, or for religion, is as agreeable to God as a garment which warmed and covered him would be to a poor man ; and that if he who labours for the good of religion makes no progress on account of the obstacles he meets with, his reward will not be the less for this before God.

While they chanted the Response, *Vocavit angelus,** she knew that choirs of angels, whose assistance is so powerful, surround the elect to defend them. But God, by His paternal Providence, sometimes suspends the effect of this protection, and permits the just to be tempted, that He may recompense them gloriously when they have gained a victory with less help from on high and from their angels.

At the Response, *Vocavit angelus Domini Abraham,* she learned that as Abraham satisfied the claims of obedience by raising his arm, and merited to be called by an angel, so, when the elect bend their minds and their wills to perform

---

* "The angel of the Lord called Abraham," Quinquagesima Sunday, v. Response, ii. Nocturn.

any painful work for the love of God, they merit
to taste at that moment the sweetness of grace,
and to be consoled by the testimony of their
own conscience. And this is a favour which the
infinite liberality of God bestows even before those
eternal recompenses which shall be given to
each according to the measure of his works. As
the Saint reflected on some trials which she had
formerly suffered, she inquired of God why she
had been thus tried by these persons. "When
the hand of a father wills to chastise his child,"
replied our Lord, "the rod cannot oppose itself.
Therefore, I desire that My elect should never
attribute their sufferings to those whom I make
use of to purify them ; but rather let them cast
their eyes on My paternal love, which would not
allow even a breath of wind to approach them
unless it fürthered their eternal salvation ; and
therefore they should have compassion on those
who stain themselves to purify them."

CHAPTER XIII.

HOW WE SHOULD OFFER OUR ACTIONS THROUGH THE SON TO THE ETERNAL FATHER.

ONE day the Saint offered a painful duty to the Eternal Father, saying: "Lord, I offer Thee this action through Thy only Son, in the power of the Holy Spirit, for Thy eternal glory." And it was made known to her that this intention gave an extraordinary value and price to her work, and elevated it above a mere human action; and that this offering was very agreeable to God the Father. And even as objects appear green when seen through green glass, or red when seen through red glass, so all that is offered to the Eternal Father through His only Son becomes most pleasing and acceptable to Him.

Of the utility of prayer when it does not produce sensible fruit.

Gertrude inquired of God what advantage some of her friends had gained by her prayers, since they did not seem better for them. The Lord instructed her by this comparison : "When a child returns from visiting an emperor, who has enriched him with vast possessions and an immense revenue, those who behold him in the weakness of childhood little imagine the treasures of which he is in possession, although those who have been present are well aware how powerful and important his wealth will render him hereafter. Do not, therefore, be surprised if you do not see the fruits of your prayers with your bodily eyes, since I dispose of them, according' to My eternal wisdom, to greater advantage. And know that the more you pray for any one, the happier they will become, because no prayer of faith can remain unfruitful, although we do not know in what manner it will fructify."

Of the eternal recompense of directing our thoughts to God.

Gertrude desired to know what advantage there was in referring our thoughts to God, and she received this instruction: that when man raises his mind to heaven by meditation or reflection, he presents, as it were, before the throne of God's glory a bright and shining mirror, in which the Lord beholds His own image with pleasure, because He is the Author and Dispenser of all good. And the more difficulty any one finds in this elevation of soul, the more perfect and agreeable this mirror appears before the Most Holy Trinity and the saints, and it will remain for the eternal glory of God and the good of this soul.

CHAPTER XIV.

WHY GOD IS PLEASED BY IMAGES OF JESUS CRUCIFIED.

ON the return of the community from a procession which had been ordered for fine weather, Gertrude heard the Son of God speak thus to His Father from a crucifix which had been carried before the procession : " Eternal Father, I come with My whole army to supplicate You, under the same form in which I reconciled You to the human race." And these words were received by the Eternal Father with as much complacence as if a satisfaction had been offered to Him which surpassed a thousand times all the sins of men. Then she beheld God the Father taking up the image of the crucifix into the clouds, with these words :

" This is the sign of the covenant which I have made with the earth." (Gen. ix.)

On another occasion, when the people were suffering exceedingly from the inclemency of the weather, the Saint often implored the mercy of God with others, but without effect. At last she addressed her Lord thus : " O charitable Lord, how canst Thou so long resist the desires of so many persons, since I, who am so unworthy of Thy goodness, have often obtained much more considerable favours merely by the confidence I have in Thee?" " Why be surprised," replied our Lord, " that a father should allow his son to ask him repeatedly for a crown, if he laid by a hundred marks of gold for him each time the request was made ? Neither should you be surprised if I defer answering your petition ; because each time that you implore My aid by the least word, or even in thought, I prepare a recompense for you in eternity of infinitely greater value than a hundred marks of gold."

CHAPTER XV.

THE VALUE AND EFFICACY OF GOOD DESIRES.

ON another occasion, as the Saint grieved in her heart that she could not form as ardent desires for the glory of God as she wished to do, she was taught by God that He is perfectly satisfied with our desires when we are not able to do more; and that they are great in proportion to our desire that they should be great. When, therefore, the heart forms a desire, or wishes to have a desire, God takes the same pleasure in abiding therein as men do in dwelling where flowers are budding forth in the spring-time. Once also, when she found herself negligent and distracted from infirmity, and, entering into herself, began to confess her fault to our Lord with humble devotion—though she feared that it would be long before she should recover the sweetness of Divine grace, of which she had been deprived—the infinite mercy of God was moved towards her, and He said to her : " My daughter, thou hast been always with Me, and all that I have is thine." Then she knew by these words that when, through frailty, we fail to refer our intention to God, His mercy still esteems our will worthy of eternal recompense, provided only that our will has not strayed from Him, and that we often make acts of contrition for our sins.

As the Saint felt an illness coming on her immediately before a festival, she desired that our Lord would preserve her health until it was over, or at least permit her to have sufficient strength to assist at it; still, she abandoned herself entirely to the will of God. Then she received this reply from the Lord : "In asking Me these things, and at the same time in submitting entirely to My will, you lead Me into a garden of delights, enamelled with flowers, which is most agreeable to Me. But I know that if I grant what you ask, and allow you to assist at these services, I shall be obliged to follow you into the place which pleases you ; whereas, if I refuse you this, and you still continue patient, you will follow Me into the place which I prefer, because I find more pleasure in you if you form good intentions in a state of suffering, than if you have devotion accompanied by pleasure."

CHAPTER XVI.

HOW WE MAY PROFIT BY THE MERIT OF OTHERS.

ERTRUDE was requested by a person, when she offered to God all the gratuitous gifts with which He had favoured her, to ask that she might have a share in their merit. As she prayed thus, she perceived this person standing before the Lord, who was seated on His throne of glory, and held in His hand a robe magnificently adorned, which He presented to her, but still without clothing her in it. The Saint, being surprised at this, said to Him : " When I made a similar offering to Thee, a few days since, Thou didst at once take the soul of the poor woman for whom I prayed to the joys of paradise ; and why, most loving Lord, dost Thou not now clothe this person with the robe which Thou hast shown her, and which she so ardently desires, through the merits of the graces Thou hast bestowed on me, though so unworthy of them?" Our Lord answered : " When anything is offered to Me for the faithful departed, I immediately use it for them, according to My natural inclination to show mercy and pardon, either for the remission of their sins, for their consolation, or for the increase of their eternal felicity, according to the condition of those for whom the offering is made. But when a similar offering is made for the living, I keep it for their benefit, because they can still increase their merit by their good works, by their good desires, and by their good will; and it is only reasonable that they should endeavour to acquire by their labour what they desire to obtain through the intercession of others.

"Therefore, if she for whom you pray desires to be clothed with your merits, she must study these three things : first, she must receive this robe with humility and gratitude—that is to say, she must acknowledge humbly that she has need of the merits of others—and she must render Me fervent thanksgivings for having deigned to supply her poverty out of their abundance; secondly, she must take this robe with faith and hope—that is, hoping in My goodness, she must believe that she will receive thereby a great assistance to her eternal salvation; thirdly, let her clothe herself in charity, exercising herself in this and in other virtues. Let all those who desire a share in the merits and virtues of others, act in like manner, if they would profit thereby."

CHAPTER XVII.

HOW OUR LORD CONSOLED ST. GERTRUDE BY OFFERING HER HIS HEART.

S it usually happens that the injuries which we receive from a friend are more difficult to bear than those which we receive from an enemy, according to the words of Scripture, "If my enemy had reviled me, I would verily have borne with it" (Ps. liv.) —Gertrude, knowing that a certain person, for whose welfare she had laboured with extreme solicitude, did not respond with the same fidelity to her care, and even, through a kind of contempt, acted contrary to what she advised, had recourse to our Lord in her affliction, who consoled her thus: " Do not be grieved, My daughter, for I have permitted this to happen for your eternal welfare, that I may the oftener enjoy your company and conversation, in which I take so much pleasure. And even as a mother who has a little child whom she loves specially, and therefore desires to have always with her, places something that will alarm her,* and

* " Larvas."

oblige her to come back into her arms when she has strayed from her; so also, desiring to have you always near Me, I permit your friends to contradict you in some things, that you may find no true fidelity in any creature, and therefore have recourse to Me with all the more eagerness, because you know that I possess the plenitude and stability of all contentment."

After this it seemed to her as if our Lord placed her in His bosom like a little child, and there caressed her in many ways; and, approaching His adorable lips to her ears, He whispered to her : " As a tender mother soothes the troubles of her little one by her kisses and embraces, so do I desire to soothe all your pain and grief by the sweet murmur of My loving words." After the Saint had enjoyed these and many other consolations for some time, our Lord offered her His Heart, and said to her : " Contemplate now, My beloved, the hidden secrets of My Heart, and consider attentively with what fidelity I have ordered all that you have ever desired of Me for your benefit and the salvation of your soul ; and see if you can accuse Me of unfaithfulness to you, even by a single word." When she had done this, she beheld our Lord crowning her with a wreath of flowers, more radiant than gold, as a reward for the trial of which we have just spoken.

Then the Saint, remembering some persons who, she knew, were tried in other ways, said to God: "Surely these persons merit to receive from Thy liberality, Father of mercies, a richer recompense, and to be adorned with more splendid ornaments, than I, since they are not assisted by the consolations which I receive, though so unworthy, and since I do not bear what happens to me with the patience I ought ?" Our Lord replied: "In these things, as in all others, I manifest the special charity and tenderness which I have for you; even as a mother who loves her only child wishes to adorn her with ornaments of gold and silver, but, knowing that she could not bear their weight, decks her with different flowers, which, without incommoding her, do not fail to add to her attractions. So, also, I moderate the rigour of your sufferings, lest you should fall under the burden, and thereby be deprived of the merit of patience."

Then, as the Saint reflected on the great care of the Divine mercy for her salvation, she began to praise Him with great gratitude; and she perceived that those flowers with which her sufferings had been mystically rewarded, expanded more and more as she returned thanks. She understood also, that the grace that God had given her, of praising Him in adversity, was as much more excellent as an ornament of solid gold is to one which has merely been gilt.

CHAPTER XVIII.

THE VALUE OF A GOOD WILL.

CERTAIN nobleman having sent to the monastery to ask the religious to found a convent, Gertrude—who was always anxious to accomplish the will of God, though she was unable to comply with this request—cast herself before a crucifix, and offered herself to God, with her whole heart, praying that His holy will might be accomplished. It seemed to her that our Lord was deeply touched by this offering, that He descended from the cross to embrace her with extreme affection and gladness, and received her with marks of ineffable joy—even as a sick person who had been given over by the physician would receive a remedy which he had long desired, and which he hoped might

restore his health—and having then gently approached her to the adorable Wound of His Side,
He said to her: "You are welcome, My beloved ;
you are the balm of My wounds, and the sweetener
of all my griefs." Gertrude knew by these
words that when any one abandons his will
without reserve to the good pleasure of God,
whatever adversity may be impending, our Lord
receives it as if He had anointed His wounds, even
at the very hour of His Passion, with the most
precious and healing ointments.

After this, as Gertrude prayed, she began to
think of many things by which she hoped to
procure the glory of God and the advancement
of religion. But after a time she reproached
herself for these reflections, which perhaps could
never bear any fruit, because she was so weak
that she seemed more likely to die than to be
able to undertake any laborious work. Then
the Lord Jesus appeared to her in the midst of
her soul, radiant with glory, and adorned with
roses and fair lilies; and He said to her: "Behold,
how I am adorned by your good will, even as I
was by the stars and the golden candlesticks,
in the midst of which St. John, in the Apo-
calypse, declares that he saw the Son of Man
standing, and having seven stars in His right

hand ; and know that I have received as much pleasure from the other thoughts of your heart as from this sweet and agreeable garland of lilies and roses."

" O God of my heart !" exclaimed the Saint, " why dost Thou embarrass my soul with so many different desires, which are all without effect.? since it is so short a time since Thou didst give me the thought and desire of receiving extreme unction, and disposed my soul to receive it by filling me with such joy and consolation. And now, on the contrary, Thou dost make me desire the establishment of a new monastery, although I am still so weak that I am scarcely able to walk." " I do this," replied our Lord, " to accomplish what I have said at the commencement of this book, that 'I had given you to be the light of the Gentiles ;' that is, to enlighten many people : therefore it is necessary that your book should contain information on many subjects, for the consolation and instruction of others. And as two persons who love each other often find pleasure in conversing on subjects which do not specially concern them—as a friend often proposes to his friend the most difficult and intricate questions —so do I take pleasure in proposing many things to My elect which will never happen to them, in order to prove their love and fidelity for Me, and to reward them for many purposes which they cannot carry into effect, counting all their good intentions, as if they had been carried into action.   So I inclined your will to desire death; and, consequently, made you feel this wish to receive extreme unction.   And I have preserved in the depth of My heart, for your eternal salvation, all that you have done in thought or act to prepare yourself for this Sacrament.   Thus you may understand these words : ' The just man, if he be prevented with death, shall be in rest.'   For if you were deprived of this Sacrament by sudden death, or if you received it after you had lost consciousness—which often happens to my elect—you would not suffer any loss thereby, because all the preparation for death which you have made for so many years is preserved in the unfading spring-time of My Divinity, where, by My coöperation, it always remains green and flourishing, and fructifying for your eternal salvation."

CHAPTER XIX.

OF THE LANGUOR CAUSED BY DIVINE LOVE.

SOON after, during the seventh illness of the Saint, as her mind was occupied with God, on a certain night our Lord approached her, and said to her, with extreme sweetness and charity : " Tell Me, My beloved, that you languish for love of Me." She replied : " How can I, a poor sinner, presume to say that I languish for love to Thee ?" Our Lord answered : " Whoever offers himself willingly to suffer anything in order to please Me, he truly glorifies Me, and, glorifying Me, tells Me that he languishes for love of Me ; provided that he continues patient, and that he never turns his eyes away from Me." " But what advantage canst Thou gain from this assurance, my beloved Lord ?" inquired the Saint. The Lord answered : " This assurance imparts joy to My Divinity, glory to My Humanity, pleasure to My eyes, and satisfaction to My ears. Further, the unction of My love is so powerfully moved thereby, that I am compelled to heal the contrite heart—that is to say, those who desire this

grace; to preach to those who are in captivity
—that is, to pardon sinners; to open the door
to those who are in prison—that is, to release
the souls in purgatory."

Gertrude then said to the Lord: "Father of
mercies, after this sickness, which is the seventh
that I have had, wilt Thou not restore me to
my former health?" Our Lord replied: "If I
had made known to you at the commencement
of your first illness that you would have to endure seven, perhaps you would have given way
to impatience through human frailty. So, also,
if I now promised you that this would be the
last sickness, the hope with which you would
look forward to its termination might lessen
your merit. Therefore the paternal providence
of My uncreated wisdom has wisely ordained
that you should remain ignorant on both subjects, that you might be obliged to have recourse
to Me continually with your whole heart, and to
commend your troubles, whether exterior or interior, to My fidelity; since I watch over you
so faithfully and lovingly, that I would not permit you to be tried beyond your strength, knowing how much your patience can bear. This
you can easily understand, if you remember how
much weaker you were after your first sickness

than you are now after you seventh; for although human reason might have considered this impossible, yet nothing is impossible to my Divine omnipotence."

CHAPTER XX.

HOW THE PLEASURE OF THE SENSES DEPRIVES OF SPIRITUAL PLEASURES.

AS the Saint one day reflected on the arrangements of Providence, by which some are filled with consolation, while others experience only dryness, God made known to her that He had created the human heart to contain pleasure, as a vase contains water. But if this vase lets out the water by little holes, it soon becomes empty; or if any water remains, it will eventually dry up. So, if the human heart, when filled with spiritual delights, pours itself out through the bodily senses, by seeing, hearing, &c., it will at last become empty, and incapable of tasting the pleasures which are found in God, as each may know by his own experience. If we give a glance or say a word without reflection, it passes away like water emptied from a vessel. But if we do ourselves violence for the love of God, celestial sweetness will so increase in our hearts that they will seem too small to contain it. Thus, when we learn to restrain the pleasures of the senses, we begin to find pleasure in God; and the more this victory costs us, the more joy we find in God.

Once, as the Saint was exceedingly troubled about a matter of little consequence, and offered her trouble to God, for His eternal glory, at the moment of the Elevation, it seemed to her that our Lord drew her soul by the Host as if by a ladder, until He made it repose on His bosom, and then He spoke thus lovingly to her: "In this sacred couch you shall be exempt from every care; but whenever you leave it, your heart will be filled with a bitterness as an antidote against evil."

CHAPTER XXI.

HOW THE SOUL IS PURIFIED AND EMBELLISHED BY THE MERITS OF JESUS CHRIST.

ON the Sunday *Invocabit*,* as Gertrude felt unable to receive the Body of our Lord, she besought Him with her whole heart to supply, by His forty days' fast, for the dispensations which her infirmity obliged her to accept. Then the Son of God rose up and knelt before His Father, with a joyful countenance, saying : " I, who am Thy only Son, coëternal and consubstantial with Thee, know, by My inscrutable wisdom, the defects of human weakness as man could not know ; therefore do I abundantly compassionate this weakness, and, desiring to supply for it perfectly, I offer Thee, O holy Father, the restraints of My blessed Mouth, in atonement for all sins of omission and commission of which the tongues of men are guilty ; I offer Thee, O just Father, the restraints of My Ears for all their sins of hearing ; I offer Thee the restraints of My Eyes for all their sins com-

---

* *Invocabit:* "He shall call upon Me, and I will hear him," &c. Introit for the First Sunday in Lent.

mitted by seeing ; I offer Thee the restraints of My Hands and Feet for all the sins of those members. Lastly, I offer to Thy Majesty, O most loving Father, My Divine Heart for all their sins of thought, desire, or will."

Then the Saint stood before God the Father, clothed in a red and white garment, and adorned with many ornaments. The white robe indicated the innocence conferred on her soul by the mortifications of Christ ; the red signified the merits of His fasts ; and the diversity of ornaments, the many ways and exercises by which our Lord laboured for our eternal salvation. Then the Eternal Father took this soul thus adorned, and placed it at a banquet between Himself and His only Son. On the one side, the splendour of the Divine omnipotence overshadowed her, to enhance her apparel and her dignity ; on the other side, she was illuminated by the light of the inscrutable wisdom of God the Son, which had adorned and embellished her with the treasures and perfections of His life. Between these two lights there was an opening,* through which might be seen the humble sentiments which this soul had of her baseness and

* "Rima."

defects ; and her humility pleased God so much, that it won for her the tenderest affection of this Almighty King.

Then our Lord placed before St. Gertrude the three victories,* which are mentioned in the Gospel of the day, under the form of different kinds of food, that they might serve her as an antidote against the three vices to which men are most subject—namely, delectation, consent, and concupiscence. First, He manifested to her the signal victory which He had gained over the devil, who tempted Him to the pleasure of eating, when he asked Him to change the stones into bread, and our Lord wisely answered him, that man doth not live by bread alone ; and He desired her to offer it to God, in satisfaction for all the sins which she might have committed through love of pleasure, and to obtain strength to resist such temptations for the time to come. For the more we yield to temptations, the less capable we are of resisting them ; and each may thus offer our Lord's victory for their own needs. Our Lord then gave her His second victory for

* Our Lord's three victories over His threefold temptations in the wilderness, related in the Gospel for the First Sunday of Lent, Matt. iv. 1–11 ; the Epistle is 2 Cor. vi. 1–10.

the remission of all the sins which she might have committed by consent, and to obtain grace for the future to resist these temptations efficaciously; and each may also offer this victory for the same end, and with the same advantage, to obtain from God the pardon of all sins of thought, word, or act, and grace to avoid falling for the time to come. Lastly, our Lord gave her His third victory as a remedy against avarice, which desires the goods and advantages of earth, and to obtain strength to resist this temptation.

During the Epistle at Mass, the Saint applied herself to noting the virtues mentioned therein, which she thought might be most useful to practise or to teach others; and as she felt she needed the gift of understanding, she said to the Lord: "Teach me, O Beloved, which of these virtues will please Thee best; for, alas! I am not specially earnest in any." Our Lord replied: "Observe that the words *In Spiritu Sancto* ('in the Holy Ghost') occur in the middle of these victories. As, therefore, the Holy Spirit is a goodwill,* study above all things to have this goodwill, for you will gain more by it than by any other virtue, and it will obtain for you the per-

---

* "Spiritus Sanctus est bona voluntas."

fection of all virtue. For whoever has a perfect will to praise Me, if he could, more than all the world, or to love Me, thank Me, suffer with Me, or exercise himself in the most perfect manner in all kinds of virtue, will certainly be recompensed by My Divine liberality more advantageously than one who has actually performed many other things." Then the Holy Spirit appeared before Gertrude, enlightening in a marvellous manner that place where the depravity and imperfection of her soul could be seen; so that, the virtue of this Divine light having entirely removed her defects, she found herself happily immersed in the Source of eternal light.

CHAPTER XXII.

OF THE TRUE MANNER OF SPIRITUALLY PERFORMING THE CORPORAL WORKS OF MERCY.

THE second *feria* after the Sunday *Invocabit*, as these words were read in the Gospel,* " Come, ye blessed of My Father; for I was hungry," &c., St. Gertrude

* Gospel for the Monday after the First Sunday in Lent, Matt. xxv. 31–46.

said to our Lord: " O my Lord, since we cannot feed the hungry and give drink to the thirsty, because our Rule forbids us to possess anything of our own, teach me how we may participate in the sweet blessings with which Thou hast promised in this Gospel to reward works of mercy." Our Lord replied : "As I am the Salvation and Life of the Soul, and as I continually hunger and thirst for the salvation of men, if you endeavour to study some words of Scripture every day for the benefit of others, you will bestow on Me a most sweet refection. If you read with the intention of obtaining the grace of compunction or devotion, you appease My thirst by giving Me an agreeable beverage to drink. If you employ yourself in recollection for an hour each day, you give Me hospitality ; and if you apply yourself daily to acquire some new virtue, you clothe Me. You visit Me when sick, by striving to overcome temptation, and to conquer your evil inclinations ; and you visit Me in prison, and solace My afflictions with the sweetest consolations, when you pray for sinners and for the souls in purgatory." He added : " Those who perform these devotions daily for My love, especially during the holy season of Lent, will most certainly receive the tenderest and most bountiful recompense which My incomprehensible omnipotence, My inscrutable wisdom, and My most loving benevolence, can bestow."

CHAPTER XXIII.

OF THE OBLATION OF THE MERITS OF JESUS CHRIST FOR THE SINS OF THE CHURCH.

ON the Sunday *Reminiscere*,* St. Gertrude, being favoured with singular marks of the love and tenderness of her Spouse, such as no human being could describe, besought our Lord to indicate some practice which might be profitable during this week. Our Lord replied : "Bring Me two good kids—I mean the souls and the bodies of all mankind."

The Saint understood from this that she was required to make satisfaction for all mankind ; and then, impelled by the Holy Ghost, she said the *Pater noster* five times, in honour of the Five Wounds of our Lord, in satisfaction for all the

---

* "Remember, O Lord, Thy compassions and Thy mercies," &c. Introit, Second Sunday in Lent.

sins which men had committed by the five senses; and three times for the sins committed by the three powers of the soul—namely, by reason, temper, and concupiscence; and for all omissions or commissions : offering this prayer with the same intention and for the same end, as our Lord had formed it in His sweetest Heart ; that is to say, in satisfaction for all the sins of frailty, ignorance, or malice which man had opposed to His omnipotent power, His inscrutable wisdom, and His overflowing and gratuitous goodness.

When Gertrude offered this prayer, our Lord appeared to take an incredible pleasure therein, and made the sign of the cross on her from her head to her feet; blessing her, and then embracing her, He led her to His Father to receive His benediction also. God the Father also received her with great condescension and magnificence, and blessed her in so ineffable a manner, that He gave her as many benedictions as He would have given to the whole world if it had been prepared to receive this favour and grace.

This prayer may be offered to God during this week to obtain the pardon of our sins and omissions, and in satisfaction for the sins of the Church, that we may obtain the effect of so salutary a benediction through the merits of Jesus

Christ, who with such condescension and goodness has deigned to be the Spouse and Head of His Church.

CHAPTER XXIV.

HOW WE MAY OBTAIN A SHARE IN THE MERITS OF THE LIFE OF JESUS CHRIST.

ON the Sunday *Oculi*,* as the Saint desired, as usual, to conform her devotions to the Church's offices, she asked our Lord to teach her how she should occupy herself during this week. He replied: " As in chanting your Office during this week you record how Joseph was sold by his brethren for twenty pieces of silver,† recite the *Pater noster* thirty-three times, and thus purchase the merit of My most holy life, which lasted for three-and-thirty years,

* *Oculi*—Introit for Third Sunday in Lent.

† The Lessons of the i. Nocturn for the Third Sunday in Lent are taken from the 37th chapter of Genesis, which details the history of Joseph sold into Egypt. In an Italian translation of 1606 it is " trenta dinari;" and in the French, " trente deniers;" two Latin editions have " xxx. denariis" also—probably a mistake of a transcriber, which has been thoughtlessly perpetuated.

during which I laboured for the salvation of men; and communicate the fruit of what you thus acquire to the whole Church, for the salvation of men and My eternal glory." As the Saint complied with this direction, she perceived in spirit that the whole Church was like a spouse adorned and embellished in a marvellous manner with the fruit of the perfect life of Jesus Christ.

CHAPTER XXV.

THE SAINT IS INSTRUCTED HOW TO ATONE FOR THE SINS OF THE CHURCH.

ON *Lœtare* Sunday, as the Saint sought for some instruction from our Lord how to spend this week, He replied to her: "Bring those persons to Me whose souls you prepared seven days since, through the virtue of My life; for they must eat at My table." She replied: "How can I do this? For myself, however unworthy I am, I will venture to say, that if I could bring to Thee all the children of men in whom Thou dost take delight, I would willingly traverse the whole earth with bare feet from this moment until the day of judgment, and carry them in my arms to Thee, to correspond, in some manner, with Thy infinite love. And were it possible for me to do so, I would divide my heart into as many portions as there are men living in the world, to impart to each a share in the good-will which is most pleasing to Thy Divine Heart." Our Lord replied : "Your good-will suffices and satisfies Me perfectly." Then she beheld the whole Church marvellously adorned and presented to the Lord, who said to her : " You shall serve all this multitude to-day."

Then Saint Gertrude cast herself at the feet of her Spouse, being divinely inspired, and kissed the Wound of His Left Foot, in satisfaction for all the sins which had ever been committed in the Church, by thought, will, or desire ; beseeching our Lord to give her for this purpose the perfect satisfaction which He had made by washing away the sins of all men. Our Lord then imparted this grace to her under the form of bread, which she immediately offered Him with thanksgiving, and which He received with great condescension, and, raising His eyes to His Eternal Father, blessed it, and gave it to her to distribute to His Church. Then she kissed the Right Foot of our Lord, in satisfaction for the omissions of the faithful in good thoughts and desires, and in good-will; beseeching our Lord to impart to them a share in that perfect satisfaction which He had made for the debts of all men. Then she kissed the Wound of the Left Hand, in satisfaction for the sins of the whole world, whether committed by word or deed; beseeching our Lord to grant the merits of His words and actions for this intention. She then kissed the Wound of the Right Hand, in satisfaction for the omissions of good words and works; beseeching our Lord to impart the plenitude and perfection of His actions to supply what was deficient in His Church.

At each of these offerings she received bread, and returned each portion to our Lord, who blessed it, and gave it to her to distribute to the Church. Then she approached the loving Wound of the Side of Jesus, and, embracing it with her whole heart, besought Him to supply to His Spouse, the Church, what was wanting to her perfection and merits, even after He had so perfectly expiated her sins, and so fully supplied for her defects; so that His Divine Life— which is agreeable in the sight of God the Father, and shines with such surpassing brightness—might become her crown and everlasting beatitude. Then the Saint rejoiced for the grace which God had given her, and distributed these loaves as one would a dessert after a meal, and said to our Lord : " Ah, Lord ! what wilt Thou give me for Thy Spouse the Church, instead of the fish which are mentioned in this day's Gospel ? " * Our Lord replied : " I will give you all My most perfect actions to distribute to those who have neglected to serve Me as much as they ought to have done, and all the most noble actions of My soul to atone for their coldness and want of fervour in praising Me for the benefits which they have received from. Me."

By the loaves which our Lord presented to the Saint, she understood that whenever any one performs a good action for God—even should it be only to say a *Pater noster*, or *Ave Maria*, or any other prayer for the Church—that the Son of God receives it as if it were the fruit of His Holy Humanity, and offers it to God His Father, blessing it and multiplying it by this benediction, so that it may be distributed

* Gospel for Fourth Sunday in Lent, John, vi. 1-15, which relates the miraculous multiplication of the five loaves and the two fishes, and so renders the mystical offering of the five loaves given to the Saint, in peculiar harmony with the offices of the day.

for the good and advancement of the whole
Church.

This devotion may be performed by any one
who says five *Pater nosters* in honour of our
Lord's Five Wounds, kissing them in spirit, and
praying for all sinners who are in the bosom of
the Church, to obtain the remission of their
sins and negligences, if they hope firmly to
receive this grace from the Divine goodness.

CHAPTER XXVI.

HOW THE BEATITUDE AND GLORY OF ST. BENE-
DICT WAS SHOWN TO ST. GERTRUDE.

ON the Feast of the glorious father St.
Benedict, St. Gertrude assisted at Matins with special devotion to honour so
excellent a father ; and she beheld him in
spirit, standing in the presence of the effulgent
and ever-peaceful Trinity, radiant with glory.
His countenance was full of majesty and beauty ;
his habit shone surpassingly ; while bright and
living roses seemed to spring forth from his

limbs, each rose producing another, and these others, the last surpassing the first in fragrance and beauty, so that our holy father, blessed both by grace and by name, being thus adorned, gave the greatest pleasure to the adorable Trinity and the heavenly court, who rejoiced with him because of his beatitude. The roses which thus sprang forth from him signified the exercises which he had used to subjugate his flesh to his spirit, and all the holy actions which he had performed, and also those of all whom he had drawn by his persuasions or induced by his example to leave the world and live under regular discipline, who following him in this royal road, had attained, or will yet attain, to the port of the celestial country and to life eternal, each of whom is a subject of particular glory to this great patriarch ; and for which all the saints praise God, and congratulate him continually.

St. Benedict also carried a sceptre, which was marvellously embellished on each side with precious stones of great brilliancy. As he held it in his hand, the side which was turned towards him emitted a glorious light, which indicated the happiness of those who had embraced his Rule and amended their lives, and on their account God overwhelmed him with inconceivable joy. On the side which was turned towards God, the Divine justice shone forth which had been magnified in the condemnation of those who had been called to this holy Order, but who had rendered themselves unworthy of it, and therefore had been condemned to eternal flames; for it is just that he whom God has called to the holiest of Orders, should be most severely punished if he lives an evil life.

Now, as St. Gertrude offered the blessed father the recital of the entire Psalter in his honour, on the part of the community, he appeared exceedingly rejoiced, and he offered the verdure with which he was adorned for the welfare of those who sought his protection with pure hearts, and walked in his footsteps by faithful observance of his Rule.

While the Response, *Grandi Pater fiducia morte stetit preciosa*, was chanted, St. Gertrude said to him : " Holy father, what special reward have you received for your glorious death ?" He replied : " Because I gave up my last breath while I was in prayer, I now emit a breath of such surpassing sweetness, that the saints delight to be near me." Then she besought him, by his glorious death, to assist each religious of that monastery in their last hour. The venerable father replied : " All who invoke me, remembering the glorious end with which God honoured me, shall be assisted by me at their death with such fidelity, that I will place myself where I see the enemy most disposed to attack them ; thus, being fortified by my presence, they will escape the snares which he lays for them, and depart happily and peacefully to the enjoyment of eternal beatitude."

PART II.

PART II.

Revelations of the Love of the Heart of Jesus in the Most Holy Sacrament.

————

ALL the Revelations with which our dear Lord favoured this most favoured of His Saints concerning the Sacrament of Love, manifest yet more and more the depth of tenderness which He reserves for His chosen in this surpassing gift. He will have all approach Him. His Heart is open to the weakest and even to the most imperfect, if their imperfections are not wilful; nay, He even tells His servant that there are some who absent themselves from this Banquet, because they do not see the " tenderness of His Paternal Heart." Who shall tell us the tenderness which gives itself as food, and grieves only when its creatures will not be fed ?

CHAPTER I.

HOW THE HEART OF JESUS DESIRES US TO
COMMUNICATE, NOTWITHSTANDING OUR UN-
WORTHINESS.

S Gertrude prepared herself for Communion on the Feast of the Holy Innocents,
she found herself distracted by a crowd
of importunate thoughts; and having implored
the Divine assistance, our Lord, in His exceeding mercy, spoke thus to her: "If any one,
when encompassed by temptation, throws himself on My protection with a firm hope, he is of
the number of those of whom I can say: 'One
is My dove, chosen amongst a thousand; he
has pierced My Divine Heart with one glance
of his eye,' so that if I thought I could not
assist him, My heart would be so desolate
that even all the joys of heaven could not alle-
viate My grief, because he is a part of My Body,
and is united to My Divinity; and I am ever
the advocate of My elect, full of compassion for
their every need."

"Lord," replied St. Gertrude, "how is it
that Thy immaculate Body, in which Thou never

hadst any contradiction, enables Thee to compassionate our many weaknesses?" He replied: "You may easily convince yourself of this. Has not My Apostle said : ' It behoved Him in all things to be made like unto His brethren, that He might be able to succour them also that are tempted?'" He added : "This eye of My beloved, which pierces My Heart, is the confidence which she ought to have in Me—that I know, that I am able, and that I am willing to assist her faithfully in all her miseries; and this confidence has such power over My goodness, that it is not possible for me to abandon her." "But, Lord," replied the Saint, "since confidence is so great a gift that none can have it unless Thou dost bestow it, what merit have those who are deprived of it?" He replied : "Each can at least overcome his diffidence, in some degree, by the testimony of Scripture, and say, if not with his whole heart, at least with his lips: ' If I should be cast into hell, Thou, O Lord, wilt deliver me;' and again, 'Although He should kill me, I will trust Him.'"

Gertrude, having one day heard a sermon on the justice of God, was so overcome by fear, that she dared not approach this Divine Sacrament ; but God, in His mercy, reassured her by these words: " If you will not look with the eyes of your soul on the many mercies which I have bestowed on you, open at least the eyes of your body, and behold Me before you enclosed in a little pyx, and know assuredly that the rigour of My justice is even thus limited within the bounds of the mercy which I exercise towards men in the dispensation of this Sacrament."

On a similar occasion, the sweetness of Divine goodness urged her to a participation in the Holy Mysteries, by these words : " Consider in how small a space I give you My entire Divinity and My Humanity. Compare the size* of this with the size of the human body, and judge then of the greatness of My love. For as the human body surpasses My Body in size—that is to say, the quantity of the species of bread under which My Body is contained—so My mercy and charity in this Sacrament reduce Me to this state, that the soul which loves Me is in some sort above Me, as the human body is greater than My Body."

On another day, as she received the saving Host, our Lord addressed her thus : " Consider that the priest who gives you the Host touches

* Quantitatem.

it directly with his hands, and that the vestments with which he is clothed, out of respect, do not reach beyond his arms ; this is to teach you, that although I regard with pleasure all that is done for my glory, as prayers, fasts, vigils, and other like works of piety, still (those who have little understanding will not comprehend it) the confidence with which the elect have recourse to Me in their weakness touches Me far more sensibly : even as you see My Flesh is nearer to the hands of the priest than his vestments."

As Gertrude was about to communicate, and feared she was not sufficiently prepared, though the moment was at hand, she addressed her soul thus : " Behold, thy Spouse calls thee ; and how canst thou dare to appear before Him without being adorned as thou shouldst be ?" Then, reflecting more and more on her unworthiness—entirely distrusting herself, and placing her confidence in the mercy of God alone—she said to herself : " Why defer longer ? since, even had I a thousand years, I could not prepare as I ought, having nothing which could serve to promote the right dispositions in me. But I will meet Him with confidence and humility ; and when my Lord beholds me from afar, He can fill me with all the grace and the attractions with which His love desires that I should appear before Him." And, approaching the Holy Mysteries in this disposition, she thought only of her negligences and imperfections. But as she advanced, she perceived our Lord regarding her with an eye of compassion, or rather of love, and sending her His innocence, that she might be adorned therewith as with a white garment. He gave her His humility, which made Him converse with creatures so utterly unworthy of such a favour; and this served her for a purple tunic. He filled her with that hope which would make her sigh ardently for Him whom she loved, to add the beauty of green to her garments. He presented her with His love of souls for a vestment of gold. He inspired her with the joy which He takes in the hearts of the faithful for a crown of precious stones. And, lastly, He gave her for sandals that confidence with which He deigned to rest on the inconstancy of human frailty, and which made Him find His delights with the children of men. And thus she was worthy to be presented to God.

CHAPTER II.

OUR LORD APPEARS TO ST. GERTRUDE UNDER THE FORM OF A PELICAN.

AFTER her Communion, as she recollected herself interiorly, our Lord appeared to her under the form of a pelican, as it is usually represented, piercing its heart with its beak. Marvelling at this, she said: "My Lord, what wouldst Thou teach me by this vision?" "I wish," replied our Lord, "that you would consider the excess of love which obliges Me to present you with such a gift ; for after having thus given Myself, I would rather remain dead in the tomb, so to speak, than deprive a soul who loves Me of the fruit of my liberality. Consider, also, that even as the blood which comes from the heart of the pelican gives life to its little ones, so also the soul whom I nourish with the Divine Food which I present to it, receives a life which will never end."

On another occasion, after Communion, as the Saint was considering with what circumspection she should use that tongue, honoured above all the members of the body in being the depository of the most precious mysteries of Jesus Christ, she was instructed by this comparison : That one who does not abstain from vain, idle, or sinful discourse, and who approaches the Holy Communion without repentance, is like a person who gathers a heap of stones at the threshold of his door, to throw at his guest when he comes to visit him, or beats him cruelly on the head with a rod.

Whence it is that we sometimes feel less fervour at the moment of Communion than at any other time.

As Gertrude prayed for a person who complained of having less devotion on the days on which she communicated than on others, our Lord said to her : " This has not happened by chance, but by a particular Providence, which inspires feelings of devotion at unexpected times, to elevate the heart of man, which is so enslaved by the body ; but on festivals and at the time of Communion I withdraw this grace, preferring to occupy the hearts of My elect with good desires or humility ; and this may be more advantageous to their welfare than the grace of devotion."

CHAPTER III.

HOW ST. GERTRUDE PREPARED FOR HOLY COMMUNION.

AS the Saint was about to communicate on one occasion, she felt grieved that she had not made sufficient preparation, and she besought the Blessed Virgin and all the saints to offer to God for her all the dispositions which each had entertained in receiving the various graces which had been granted to them. She then besought our Lord Jesus Christ that He would be pleased also to offer for her the perfection with which He appeared on the day of His Ascension, when He presented Himself to God the Father and entered into eternal glory. Afterwards she desired to know of what avail this prayer had been to her, and our Lord replied : " It has enabled you to appear before the whole court of heaven with all the ornaments you have desired." He added : "Why should you distrust Me, who am all-powerful and all-merciful, since there is not one upon earth who could not clothe his friend in his own ornaments and garments, and thereby make him appear as gloriously attired as himself?"

As she remembered afterwards that she had promised to communicate that day for some persons who had recommended themselves to her prayers, she besought God with great fervour to grant them the fruit of this Sacrament, and received this reply : "I will grant them this favour ; but I leave it to their free will to avail themselves of it as they wish." She then inquired how these souls should be prepared to receive this grace, and our Lord answered : "Whenever, from this time, they turn to Me with a pure heart and a perfect will, invoking the assistance of My grace, if only by a single word or the least sigh, they will immediately appear clothed with the ornaments that you have obtained for them by your prayers."

Once, also, as the Saint was about to communicate, she said : "O Lord, what wilt Thou give me ?" "I will give Myself to thee entirely," He replied, "with all the virtue of My Divinity, even as My Virgin Mother received Me." "But what shall I gain by this?" inquired Gertrude, "more than those persons who received Thee yesterday with me, and who will not receive Thee to-day, since Thou dost always give Thyself entirely and without reserve?" Our Lord replied: "If people in the world honour one who has been a consul twice more than a person who has only once filled that office, how shall he fail of greater glory in eternity who has received Me more frequently on earth?" Then she exclaimed, sighing: "How far above me in beatitude will those priests be who communicate every day to fulfil the duties of their ministry!" "It is true," replied our Lord, "that those who celebrate worthily shall shine in great glory; but the love of him who communicates with pleasure should be judged of very differently from the exterior magnificence which appears in this mystery. There will be one reward for him who has approached with desire and love; there will be another for him who approaches with fear and reverence; and another for him who is very diligent in his preparation. But those who habitually celebrate through custom only, shall have no share in My gifts."

CHAPTER IV.

OF THE VALUE AND IMPORTANCE OF SPIRITUAL COMMUNION.

THIS holy spouse of Jesus Christ had usually an extreme and ardent desire to receive the Body of Christ, and it happened that once, when she prepared for Communion with more than ordinary devotion, she found herself so weak on Sunday night, that she feared she would not be able to communicate; but, according to her usual custom, she consulted her Lord, to know what would be most pleasing to Him. He replied: "Even as a spouse who was already satisfied with a variety of viands would prefer remaining near his bride to sitting at table with her, so would I prefer that you should deprive yourself of Communion through holy prudence, on this occasion, rather than approach it." "And how, my loving Lord, can You say that You are thus satiated?" The Lord replied: "By your moderation in speech, by your guard over your senses, by all your desires, by all your prayers, by all the good dis-

positions with which you have prepared to receive
My adorable Body and Blood—these are to Me
as the most delicious food and refreshment."

When she came to Mass, though still in a
state of extreme weakness, and had prepared
for spiritual Communion, she heard the sound of
a bell, announcing the return of a priest who had
gone to a village to give Communion to a sick
person. "O Life of my soul!" she exclaimed,
"how gladly would I receive Thee spiritually, if
I had time to prepare myself worthily!" "The
looks of My Divine mercy," replied the Lord,
"will impart to you the necessary preparation;"
and at the same time it seemed to the Saint that
the Lord cast a look upon her soul like a ray of
sunlight, saying: "I will fix My eyes upon thee"
(Ps. xxxi.). From these words she understood
that the look of God produces three effects in
our souls, similar to those that the sun produces
in our bodies, and that the soul ought to prepare
in three ways to receive it. First, the glance of
Divine mercy searches the soul, and purifies it
from every stain, making it whiter than snow;
and we obtain this favour by a humble acknow-
ledgment of our defects. Secondly, this look of
mercy softens the soul, and prepares it to receive
spiritual gifts, even as wax is softened by the

heat of the sun, and becomes capable of receiving any impression ; and the soul acquires this by a pious intention. Thirdly, the glance of Divine mercy on the soul makes it fruitful in the different flowers of virtue, even as the sun produces and ripens different sorts of fruit ; and the third effect is obtained by a faithful confidence, which causes us to abandon ourselves entirely to God, confiding assuredly in the superabundance of His mercy, believing that all things will contribute to our eternal welfare, whether they appear favourable or adverse. Then, as some of the community communicated at Mass, our Divine Lord appeared to give Himself to each with His own Hand, making the sign of the cross as the priest does. The Saint, marvelling at this, said to Him : " Lord, have not those who have received Thee in this Sacrament obtained greater grace than I, whom Thou hast gratuitously favoured with so many benefits ?" " Who is esteemed most worthy," replied our Lord, "he who is adorned with pearls and precious stones, or he who has an immense treasure of pure gold hidden in his house ?" making her understand by these words, that while he who communicates sacramentally receives without doubt immense grace, both spiritually and corporally, as the Church believes, still, he who abstains from receiving the Body of Christ through obedience and holy discretion, and purely for the glory of God, and who, being inflamed with Divine love, communicates spiritually, merits to receive a benediction like that given to the saint, and obtains from God more abundant fruit, although the order and secret of this conduct is entirely hidden from the eyes of men.

Once as the sisters communicated at the Mass, our Lord placed Gertrude tenderly at the loving Wound of His Side, and said to her : "Since discretion obliges you to abstain from receiving Me corporally in the Sacrament, drink now from My Heart the sweet influences of My Divinity." Having drunk of this torrent of sweetness and delight, as she thanked our Lord devoutly for it, she saw all those who had communicated that day standing in the presence of the Lord, who gave to each a marvellously beautiful habit, and a special gift, which enabled them to prepare themselves worthily for Communion. As they obtained these great favours through the merits of Gertrude, they also offered to our Lord in their turn the advantages which they had received through her, for the increase of her glory and merit. From this she understood that those who dispose themselves for Holy Communion by particular prayers and devotions, and who nevertheless abstain for good reasons, as through obedience or humility, are replenished by God with the torrent of Divine delights; while their preparation for Communion contributes to prepare others, and the fruit which others derive thereby returns to their advantage. Then St. Gertrude exclaimed : " O Lord, if it is true that those who abstain thus from communicating receive such great fruit, is it, then, more advantageous to abstain ?" Our Lord replied: " By no means ; for those who approach the Sacrament for love of My glory receive the food of My Divine Body as the delicious nectar of the Divinity, and are adorned with the incomparable splendour of My Divine virtues." " Lord," inquired the Saint, " what will happen to those who abstain from Communion on account of their negligences, and yet pass the day in the same negligences ?" He replied : " They render themselves still more unworthy of Communion, and they deprive themselves of the fruit of the Communions made on that day throughout the Church." Then the Saint continued : " Tell me, I beseech Thee, O Lord, why it happens that certain souls, who judge themselves unworthy of Communion, and apply themselves less earnestly to prepare for it, are nevertheless pressed by so ardent a desire to receive Thy sacred Body, that it grieves them exceedingly to abstain on the days appointed for receiving it?" Our Lord replied : " This happens to them by a special grace of My sweet Spirit ; as a king, who is always accustomed to the court, naturally prefers the pleasure which he always enjoys there, to the satisfaction which others find in roaming through the streets and squares."

CHAPTER V.

HOW AGREEABLE FREQUENT COMMUNION IS TO THE HEART OF JESUS.

 CERTAIN person, moved by a zeal for justice, sometimes exclaimed against those whom she thought approached the Holy Communion with too little preparation and fervour, and rendered them so fearful, that they dared not communicate. On this account, as Gertrude prayed for this person, and inquired how our Lord received her zeal, He replied :

" Since I find My delight in dwelling with the
children of men, and have left them this Sacrament, by an excess of love, for a remembrance
of Me, that by this they may remember Me frequently ; and, finally, have obliged Myself to
remain in this mystery until the consummation
of ages—all who, by their words or persuasions,
drive away those who are not in mortal sin, and
thus hinder and interrupt the delight which I
find in them, act like a severe master, who forbids the children of the king to speak to those
of their own age who may be poor or beneath
them in rank, because he considers it more correct that his pupils should receive the honour
due to their dignity than to permit them this
enjoyment."   " But, Lord," inquired the Saint,
" if this person formed a firm resolution not to
commit this fault any more, wouldst Thou not
pardon her for the past ?"   " I would not only
pardon her," our Lord replied : " but her action
would be as agreeable to Me as it would be to
the king's son if his master allowed him to play
with those children from whom he had pre-
viously driven him away with such severity."

CHAPTER VI.

OUR LORD SHOWED HIS HEART TO ST. GERTRUDE.

JESUS CHRIST once appeared to the Saint, and, showing her His Heart, said to her: "My beloved, give Me your heart:" and as she presented it to Him with profound respect, it seemed to her that He united it to His by a canal which reached to the ground, through which He poured forth abundantly the effusions of His infinite grace, saying to her : "Henceforth I shall use your heart as a canal through which I will pour forth the impetuous torrents of mercy and consolation which flow from My loving Heart on all those who shall dispose themselves to receive it, by having recourse to you with humility and confidence."

Let us, then, have recourse, with confidence, to this favoured Saint, through whom we may obtain all we desire from the Heart of God.

CHAPTER VII.

HOW GERTRUDE HEARD MASS IN ECSTASY.

ON *Gaudete* Sunday, as St. Gertrude prepared to communicate at the first Mass, which commences *Rorate*, she complained to our Lord that she could not hear Mass; but our Lord, who compassionates the afflicted, consoled her, saying: "Do you wish, My beloved, that I should say Mass for you?" Then, being suddenly rapt in spirit, she replied: "I do desire it, O Beloved of my soul; and I most ardently beseech Thee to grant me this favour." Our Lord then entoned the *Gaudete in Domino semper*, with a choir of saints, to incite this soul to praise and rejoice in Him; and as He sat on His royal throne, St. Gertrude cast herself at His Feet, and embraced them. Then He chanted the *Kyrie eleison* in a clear and loud voice, while two of the princes of the choir of Thrones took her soul and brought it before God the Father, where she remained prostrate.

At the first *Kyrie eleison*, He granted to her the remission of all the sins which she had contracted through human frailty ; after which the angels raised her up on her knees. At the second, He pardoned her sins of ignorance ; and she was raised up by these princes, so that she stood before God. Then two angels of the choir of Cherubim led her to the Son of God, who received her with great tenderness. At the first *Christe eleison*, the Saint offered our Lord all the sweetness of human affection, returning it to Him as to its Source ; and thus there was a wonderful influx of God into her soul, and of her soul into God, so that by the descending notes the ineffable delights of the Divine Heart flowed into her ; and by the ascending notes, the joys of her soul flowed back to God. At the second *Christe eleison*, she experienced the most ineffable delights, which she offered to our Lord. At the third *Christe eleison*, the Son of God extended His Hands, and bestowed on her all the fruit of His most holy life and conversation.

Two angels of the choir of Seraphim then presented her to the Holy Spirit, who penetrated the three powers of her soul. At the first *Kyrie eleison*, He illuminated her reason with the glorious light of Divine knowledge, that she might always know His will perfectly. At the second

Kyrie eleison, He strengthened the irascible* part of her soul to resist all the machinations of her enemies, and to conquer every evil. At the last *Kyrie eleison*, He inflamed her love, that she might love God with her whole heart, with her whole soul, and with her whole strength. It was for this reason that the choir of Seraphim, which is the highest order in the heavenly hosts, presented her to the Holy Ghost, who is the Third Person of the Most Holy Trinity, and that the Thrones presented her to God the Father, manifesting† that the Father, Son, and Holy Ghost, are One God, equal in glory, co-eternal in majesty, living and reigning perfect Trinity through endless ages.

The Son of God then rose from His royal throne, and, turning towards God the Father, intoned the *Gloria in excelsis*, in a clear and sonorous voice. At the word *Gloria*, He extolled the immense and incomprehensible omnipotence of God the Father; at the words *in excelsis*, He praised His profound wisdom; at *Deo*, He honoured‡ the inestimable and indescribable sweetness of the Holy Ghost. The whole celestial court then continued in a most

---

* "Iracibilem."   † "Innuebatur."
‡ "Reverebatur."

harmonious voice, *Et in terra pax bonæ voluntatis.* Our Lord being again seated on His throne, St. Gertrude sat at His feet meditating on her own abjection, when He inclined towards her lovingly. Then she arose and stood before Him, while the Divine splendour illuminated her whole being. Two angels from the choir of Thrones then brought a throne magnificently adorned, which they placed before our Lord; two princes from the choir of Seraphim placed Gertrude thereon, and supported her on each side, while two of the choir of Cherubim stood before her bearing brilliant torches; and thus she remained before her Beloved, clothed in royal purple. When the heavenly hosts came to the words *Domine Deus Rex cœlestis,* they paused, and the Son of God continued alone chanting to the honour and glory of His Father.

At the conclusion of the *Gloria in excelsis,* the Lord Jesus, who is our true High Priest and Pontiff, turned to St. Gertrude, saying, *Dominus vobiscum, dilectu*—" The Lord be with you, beloved;" and she replied: " *Et spiritus meus tecum, prædilectu*—" And may my spirit be with Thee, O my Beloved!" After this she inclined towards the Lord, to return Him thanks for His love in uniting her spirit to His Divinity,

whose delights are with the children of men.
The Lord then read the Collect, *Deus, qui hanc
sacratissimam noctem,** which He concluded with
the words, *Per Jesum Christum filium tuum,* as
if giving thanks to God the Father for illu-
minating the soul of Gertrude, whose unworthi-
ness† was indicated by the word *noctem* (night),
which was called most holy, because she had
become marvellously ennobled by the knowledge
of her own baseness.

St. John the Evangelist then rose, and stood
between God and her soul. He was adorned
with a yellow garment, which was covered with
golden eagles. He commenced the Epistle, *Hæc
est sponsa,* and the celestial court concluded,
Ipsi gloria in sæcula. Then all chanted the
Gradual, *Specia tua,*‡ adding the Versicle, *Audi
filia et vide.* After this they commenced the *Al-
leluia.* St. Paul, the great doctor of the Church,
pointed to St. Gertrude, saying, *Æmulor enim
vos* §—" For I am jealous of you" (2 Cor. xi. 2);

* Collect for Midnight Mass at Christmas.
† "Vilitas."
‡ Gradual, Mass of Virgins; *Audi filia,* Gradual of
St. Cecilia. This Mass appears to have been composed
from several Masses.
§ Epistle, Common. of Virgins. We have not been
able to verify the prose.

and the heavenly choir sang the Prose, *Filiæ Sion exultent*. At the words *Dum non consentiret*, St. Gertrude remembered that she had been a little negligent in resisting temptations, and she hid her face in shame; but our Lord, who could not bear to behold the confusion of His chaste queen, covered her negligence with a collar of gold, so that she appeared as if she had gained a glorious victory over all her enemies.

Then another Evangelist commenced the Gospel, *Exultavit Dominus Jesus*; and these words moved the Heart of Jesus so deeply, that He arose, and extending His Hands, exclaimed aloud, *Confiteor, tibi Pater*,* manifesting the same thanksgiving and gratitude to His Father as He had done when He said the same words on earth, giving special thanks for the graces bestowed on this soul. After the Gospel He desired Gertrude to make a public profession of faith, by reciting the Creed in the name of the whole Church. When she had concluded, the choir chanted the Offertory, *Domine Deus in simplicitate*, adding,

* "I confess to Thee, O Father, Lord of heaven and earth, because Thou hast hidden these things from the wise and prudent, and revealed them to little ones." (Matt. xi. 25); Gospel Com. of Martyrs.

*Sanctificavit** Moyses.* The Heart of Jesus then appeared as a golden altar, which shone with a marvellous brightness, on which the angel guardians offered the good works and prayers of those committed to their care. The saints then approached ; and each offered his merits to the eternal praise of God, and for the salvation of St. Gertrude. The angelic princes, who had charge of the Saint, next approached, and offered a chalice of gold, containing all the trials and afflictions which she had endured either in body or soul from her infancy ; and the Lord blessed the chalice with the sign of the cross, as the priest blesses it before Consecration.†

He now entoned the words *Sursum corda.* Then all the saints were summoned to come forward, and they applied their hearts, in the form of golden pipes, to the golden altar of the Divine Heart ; and from the overflowings of this chalice, which our Lord had consecrated by His bene-

---

* *Domine Deus ;* Offertory for Dedication of a Church. The continuation is taken from the Office for Dedication.

† "The priest, elevating his eyes towards heaven, &c., . . . makes the sign of the cross over the Host and Chalice, while he says : 'Come, O Sanctifier,'" &c. See Missal, Ordinary of the Mass.

diction, they received some drops for the increase of their merit, glory, and eternal beatitude.

The Son of God then chanted the *Gratius agimus*, to the glory and honour of His Eternal Father. At the Preface, He remained silent for an hour after the words *Per Jesum Christum*, while the heavenly hosts chanted the *Dominum nostrum* with ineffable jubilation, declaring that He was their Creator, Redeemer, and the liberal Rewarder of all their good works ; and that He alone was worthy of honour and glory, praise and exaltation, power and dominion, from and over all creatures. At the words *Laudant Angeli*, all the angelic spirits ran hither and thither, exciting the heavenly inhabitants to sing the Divine praises. At the words *Adorant Dominationes*, the choir of Dominations knelt to adore our Lord, declaring that to Him alone every knee should bow, whether in heaven, on earth, or under the earth. At the *Tremunt Potestatis*, the Powers prostrated before Him to declare that He alone should be adored ; and at the *Cœli cœlorumque*, they praised God with all the angel choirs.

Then all the heavenly hosts sang together in harmonious concert the *Cum quibus et nostras ;* and the Virgin Mary, the effulgent Rose of heaven, who is blessed above all creatures, chanted the *Sanctus, sanctus, sanctus,* extolling with the highest gratitude, by these three words, the incomprehensible omnipotence, the inscrutable wisdom, and the ineffable goodness, of the ever-blessed Trinity, inciting all the celestial choirs to praise God for having made her most powerful after the Father, most wise after the Son, and most benign after the Holy Ghost. The saints then continued the *Domine Deus Sabaoth.* When this was ended, Gertrude saw our Lord rise from His royal throne, and present His blessed Heart to His Father, elevating it with His own hands, and immolating it in an ineffable manner for the whole Church. At this moment the bell rang for the Elevation of the Host in the church; so that it appeared as if our Lord did in heaven what the priest did on earth; but the Saint was entirely ignorant of what was passing in the church, or what the time was. As she continued in amazement at so many marvels, our Lord told her to recite the *Pater noster.* When she had finished, He accepted it from her, and granted to all the saints and angels, for her sake, that, by this *Pater noster,* they should accomplish everything which had ever been accomplished for the salvation of the Church and for the souls in purgatory. Then He suggested to her to pray for the Church, which she did, for all in general and for each in particular, with the greatest fervour; and the Lord united her prayer to those which He had offered Himself when in the flesh, to be applied to the Universal Church.

Then she exclaimed : "But, Lord, when shall I communicate?" And our Lord communicated Himself to her with a love and tenderness which no human tongue could describe ; so that she received the perfect fruit of His most precious Body and Blood. After this He sang a canticle of love for her, and declared to her, that had this union of Himself with her been the sole fruit of His labours, sorrows, and Passion, He would have been fully satisfied. O inestimable sweetness of the Divine condescension, who so delights Himself in human hearts, that He considers His union with them a sufficient return for all the bitterness of His Passion ! and yet, what should we not owe Him had He only shed one drop of His precious Blood for us !

Our Lord then chanted *Gaudete justi*, and all the saints rejoiced with Gertrude. Then our Lord said, in the name of the Church Militant,

*Refecti cibo,** &c.; He then saluted all the saints lovingly, saying, *Dominus vobiscum*, and thereby increased the glory and joy of all the blessed. The saints and angels then sang, for the *Missa est, Te decet laus et honor Domine*, to the glory and praise of the effulgent and ever-peaceful Trinity. The Son of God extended His royal Hand, and blessed the Saint, saying : " I bless thee, O daughter of eternal light, with this special blessing, granting you this favour, that whenever you desire to do good to any one from particular affection, they will be as much benefited above others as Isaac was above Esau when he received his father's blessing."

Then the Saint recovered from her rapture, and remained more closely united than ever to her Beloved.

* Communion, Com. of Conf. not Bishop; Mass *Os justi.*

CHAPTER VIII.

HOW GERTRUDE WAS TAUGHT TO ASSIST AT MASS IN SPIRIT.

NCE, when the Saint was confined to bed, and unable to assist at Mass, at which she had hoped to have commucated, she said to God, with a troubled spirit: " To what must I attribute my hindrance from assisting to-day at the Holy Mysteries, if not to Thy Divine Providence, my Beloved? and how shall I prepare myself to receive the Communion of Thy adorable Body and Blood, since my intention at Mass always seemed to me my best preparation?" "Since you attribute the cause to Me," replied our Lord, "to console you, I will make you hear the songs of joy with which heaven resounds when I espouse a soul.

" Hear, then, from Me, that My Blood is your redemption; meditate on those three-and-thirty years during which I laboured for you in exile, and sought only to ally Myself with you; and let this serve for the first part of Mass.

" Hear Me telling how I have dowered you with the riches of My Spirit, and that even as

I endured so much bodily labour during the three-and-thirty years in which I sought you, so also my soul feels an ineffable joy at the union and spiritual marriage which we have contracted; and let this be your consolation during the second part of Mass.

" Listen, then, to Me, while I tell you how you are replenished with My Divinity, which has the power to make you taste the purest delights and the most ravishing sweetness inwardly, whilst exteriorly you are suffering the severest pain. This will serve for the third part of Mass.

" Hear, further, how you are sanctified by My love; know that you have nothing of yourself, and that all which renders you agreeable to Me comes from Me. Occupy yourself with these thoughts during the fourth part of Mass.

"Lastly, hear that you have been united to Me in the sublimest manner; and know that, as ' all power has been given to Me in heaven and on earth,' I cannot be hindered from exalting you, as a king exalts his queen to his throne, and consequently renders her an object of respect. Rejoice, then, in reflecting on these things, and do not complain again that you have been deprived of hearing Mass."

PART III.

PART III.

The Love of the Heart of Jesus in the Sacrament of Penance.

___

CHAPTER I.

OF THE VALUE AND EFFICACY OF CONFESSION —HOW WE SHOULD CONQUER THE DIFFICULTIES WE FEEL IN APPROACHING THE SACRAMENT OF PENANCE.

THE Lord, who is ever jealous of the salvation of His elect, sometimes makes the most trifling thing appear full of difficulty, for the increase of our merit. It was with this intention that He once allowed St. Gertrude to feel the duty of confession so burdensome, that it seemed as if she could never perform this duty by her own strength. She therefore addressed herself to God with all the fervour she could command, and He replied: " Why do you not confide this confession to Me, with such confidence that you need think no more of your own labour or exertion to make it

perfect ?" She replied : " I have a full and
superabundant confidence in Thy mercy and
omnipotence, my loving Lord ; but I think it is
only just, as I have offended Thee by my sins,
that I should give Thee some tokens of my
amendment, by reflecting on the disorders of my
life in the bitterness of my soul." Our Lord
having manifested to her that her design was
agreeable to Him, Gertrude occupied herself
entirely with the recollection of her sins, and
it appeared to her as if her skin were torn in
several places, and as if it had been pierced with
thorns : then, having discovered her wounds
and miseries to the Father of Mercies as to a
wise and faithful Physician, He inclined lovingly
towards her, and said : " I will warm the bath
of confession for you by My Divine breath; and
when you have bathed yourself in it, according
to My desire, you will appear without spot before Me." Then she prepared in all haste to
plunge into this bath, saying: " Lord, I renounce
every sentiment of human respect for love of
Thee; and even should I be obliged to publish
my crimes to the whole world, I am ready to do
so." Then our Lord covered her with His
mantle, and allowed her to repose upon His
bosom until this bath was prepared for her.

When the time came for confession, she was more tried than before. " Lord," she exclaimed, " since Thy paternal love knows all I suffer about this confession, why dost Thou permit me to be weighed down by this trial ?" " Those who take a bath," replied our Lord, " are accustomed to have themselves rubbed, in order to purify themselves more completely : thus the trouble of mind which you suffer will serve to purify you." Then, having perceived on the right side of her Spouse a bath which exhaled a thick vapour, she saw on the other side a delicious garden, enamelled with flowers, of which the most remarkable were roses without thorns, of rare beauty, which emitted a sweet and vivifying odour, attracting all who approached thither. The Lord made a sign to her to enter this garden if she preferred it to the bath which she feared so much. " Not this, O Lord," she exclaimed, " but the bath which Thou hast warmed for me by Thy Divine breath." Our Lord replied : " May it avail for your eternal salvation !"

Gertrude then understood that the garden represented the interior joys of Divine grace, which expose the faithful soul to the south wind of charity, water it with the loving dew of tears, and in an instant make it whiter than

snow, assuring it not only of a general pardon
of all its faults, but even of a new increase of
merit. But she doubted not God was better
pleased that for love of Him she had chosen
what was painful, and refused what was consoling. Then, having retired to pray after her
confession, she felt a most powerful assistance
from God in this exercise; so that what He had
formerly made so painful to her now appeared
light and easy. It must be observed here, that
the soul is purified from the stain of sin princi-
pally in two manners : first, by the bitterness
of penance, which is represented under the
figure of a bath; and secondly, by the sweet
embrace of Divine love, which is figured by the
garden. Before confession, the Saint had occupied herself in contemplating the Wound of
the Left Hand, so that after this bath she might
rest therein until she could accomplish the penance enjoined by the priest. But as it was
such that she was obliged to defer it for some
time, she was extremely afflicted that she could
not converse familiarly and freely with her faithful and amiable Spouse until she had paid this
debt. Therefore, during Mass, as the priest im-
molated the Sacred Host, which truly and efficaciously blots out all the sins of men, she

offered to God thanksgiving for all that He had
done for her in the bath of penance, and in satisfaction for her faults. This the Eternal Father accepted, and received her into His bosom, where
she learned that "this Orient from on high"
had visited her in the plenitude of mercy and
truth.

On the following day, as the Saint heard Mass,
she was overcome by weariness; but the sound
of the bell aroused her, and she beheld Jesus
Christ, her Lord and King, holding a tree in
His Hand, which appeared to have been just cut
from the root, but which was covered with the
most beautiful fruit, and whose leaves shone like
so many stars, shooting forth rays of admirable
brightness; and having given of these fruits to
the Saints who composed His celestial court,
they found a marvellous sweetness therein.
Soon after, our Lord planted this tree in the
garden of her heart, that she might make it
more fruitful by cultivation, that she might repose under it and be refreshed there. Having
received this deposit, she began to pray for a
person who had persecuted her a short time
before, asking, to increase its fruitfulness, that
she might suffer again what she had already
suffered, to draw down more abundant grace on

this person. At this moment she beheld a flower, of a most beautiful colour, burst forth on the top of the tree, which promised to change into fruit if she executed her good intention. This tree was the symbol of charity, which bears not only the abundant fruit of good works, but also the flowers of good-will, and the bright leaves of holy desires. Therefore, the citizens of heaven rejoice greatly when men condescend towards their brethren, and endeavour with all their power to solace them in their needs. At the moment of the Elevation of the Host, our Lord adorned the Saint with the various graces which He had communicated to her on the preceding day.

CHAPTER II.

OF THE LOVE OF THE HEART OF JESUS IN PERMITTING THE JUST TO FALL FOR THEIR HUMILIATION.

AS the Saint prayed for a person who had abstained from receiving the Body of the Lord, fearing to be an occasion of scandal, our Lord made known His will by this comparison : " As a man who washes his hands to remove a stain, removes at the same time not only what he has seen, but also cleanses his hands perfectly; so the just are allowed to fall into some trifling faults, that they may become more agreeable to Me by their repentance and humility; but there are some who contradict My designs in this, by neglecting the interior beauty which I desire to see after their penance, thinking of the exterior, and of the judgment of men; and this they do, when they deprive themselves of the grace which they might receive in the Sacrament, from the fear of scandalizing those who do not think them sufficiently prepared."

CHAPTER III.

OF THE BENEFIT WE MAY DERIVE FROM OUR FAULTS.

ONE night, as Gertrude was occupied in examining her conscience, she remarked that she had a habit of saying " God knows," without reflection and without necessity; and having blamed herself very severely for this fault, she besought the Divine Majesty never to permit her to use His sweet name lightly

again.   Our Lord replied lovingly to her :
" Why would you deprive Me of the glory and
yourself of the immense reward which you acquire every time you perceive this fault, or any
similar one, and seriously endeavour to correct
it ?   For when any one exerts himself to overcome his faults for love of Me, he offers Me the
same testimony of fidelity and respect as a sol-
dier would do to his captain when he courage-
ously resisted his enemies in battle, overcoming
them all, and casting them to the ground with
his own arm."

After this, as the Saint rested on the bosom
of her Lord, she felt a great weakness of heart,
which she offered thus to Him : " My beloved
Spouse! I offer Thee this debilitated heart, with
all its affections and desires, that Thou mayest
take pleasure therein according to Thy will."
He replied: "I accept your offering of this weak
heart, and prefer it to a strong one ; even as the
hunter prefers what he has taken in the chase to
tame animals."

Although the infirmities of the Saint prevented
her from assisting in choir, still she often went
to listen to the Office, in order thus to exercise
her body in some manner in the service of God ;
and reflecting that she was not as attentive or

recollected as she desired, she manifested her grief to her Divine Spouse, saying to Him, with a dejected heart : " What glory canst Thou receive, my loving Lord, from my sitting here in this idle and negligent manner, paying so little attention to what is said or chanted to Thy glory?" Our Lord replied : "And what satisfaction would you not have if your friend presented you with a draught of newly made and delicious mead, which you thought would strengthen you? Be assured, then, that I find infinitely more pleasure in every word, and even every syllable, to which you listen attentively for My glory."

At the Mass which was celebrated after, Gertrude felt unable to rise at the Gospel, and she doubted whether to spare herself or not on such occasions, as she had no hope of her recovery ; but she asked God, according to her custom, what would be most for His glory. He replied: " When, for love of Me, you do anything with difficulty, and which is beyond your strength, I receive it even as if I had an absolute need of it; but when you omit anything to take due care of your body, referring all to My glory, I consider it in the same manner as an infirm person would consider some relief that it was impossible for him to do without : thus I will recompense you for both, according to the greatness of My Divine munificence.

CHAPTER IV.

OF THE RENEWAL* OF THE SEVEN SACRAMENTS
IN HER SOUL, AND OF FRATERNAL CHARITY.

AS Gertrude examined her conscience one day, she discovered some faults she was extremely anxious to confess; but as she could not have recourse to her confessor at the time, she began as usual to discover her grief to our Lord, who consoled her thus: "Why," He inquired, "are you troubled, My beloved, since I am the sovereign Priest and true Pontiff, to whom you can have recourse; and I can renew in your soul with greater efficacy the grace of the Seven Sacraments, by a single operation, than either priest or bishop could by conferring each separately? For I will baptise you in My precious Blood; I will confirm you in My victorious strength; I will espouse you in My faithful love; I will consecrate you in the perfection of My holy life; I will absolve you from all your sins by the charity of My heart; I will feed you

* Renovatione.

Myself by My overflowing tenderness, and I will feed Myself also on you; I will purify you inwardly by so powerful an anointing of the sweetness of My spirit, that all your senses and your actions will breathe the most fervent piety, which, pouring down on you like holy oil, will sanctify you more and more unto life eternal."

Once when the Saint had risen to say Matins, although in a state of extreme weakness, and had already finished the first nocturn, another religious, who was also ill, came to her, and she immediately recommenced the Matins with her, with great charity and devotion. Afterwards, being occupied with God during holy Mass, she perceived that her soul was magnificently adorned with precious stones, which emitted a most admirable brightness. Our Lord then made known to her that she had received those gifts in recompense for her humble charity in having recommenced her Matins for the convenience of a younger sister; and that she had received as many different ornaments as she had repeated words. The Saint then remembered some negligence of which she had not been able to accuse herself in confession, on account of the absence of her confessor; and as she mourned over this to our Lord, He said to her: "Why do you complain of your negligences—you who are so richly clothed with the robe of charity, which covers a multitude of sins?" "How can I console myself," she replied, "when I still perceive that I am stained by them?" But our Lord answered : "Charity not only covers sins, but, like a burning sun, consumes and annihilates the slightest imperfections, and overwhelms the soul with merit."

Gertrude once perceived that a person neglected some observances of the Rule, and feared that she would be guilty in the sight of God if she did not correct it, as she knew of it ; but she also apprehended that some who were less strict might think she interfered more than was necessary in trifling matters. This trouble, however, she offered, according to her custom, to our Lord ; who, in order to show how agreeable her devotion was to Him, said to her : " Each time that, for love of Me, you suffer this reproach, or any similar to it, I will strengthen you mightily, and will encompass you, as a city is encompassed with trenches and walls, so that no occupation will be able to distract you, or to separate you from Me ; and, further, I will add to your merit that which any one might have acquired if they had submitted themselves with humility to your admonitions."

CHAPTER V.

HOW IMPERFECTIONS OF WHICH WE FORGET TO ACCUSE OURSELVES IN CONFESSION ARE PARDONED BY GOD.

N the Feast of St. John *ante Portam Latinam*, he appeared to Gertrude; and after having caressed and consoled her in a wonderful manner, he said to her: "Do not be troubled, O elect spouse of my Lord, at the failure of your bodily strength; for what you suffer in this world is but little, and will last only for a moment, in comparison with the eternal delights which we now enjoy in heaven, and which you will soon possess with us when you enter therein; for it is the nuptial couch of your Spouse, whom you love so ardently, whom you desire with such fervour, and whom you will at last possess as you desire. Then he added: "Remember that I, who was the beloved disciple of the Lord, was still more infirm in body than you are; and nevertheless I am now, as you see, the delight and devotion of the faithful; so you also, after your death, will live in the hearts of many, and will draw many souls to

God." Then she said complainingly to St. John, that she feared she had placed an obstacle to this, because she had forgotten to confess some little faults; and when she remembered them, she could not have recourse to her confessor; and that she could not always remember them when she went to confession, on account of her extreme debility. "Do not be troubled at this, my child," replied the Saint lovingly; "for when you have prepared for a good and entire confession of your sins, and find that you cannot then have recourse to a confessor, if you forget anything in consequence of the delay, and omit to accuse yourself of it merely from a defect of memory, what you have forgotten will not fail to be effaced; and the grief you have for the omission will adorn your soul as a precious jewel, which will render it pleasing to the heavenly court."

PART IV

PART IV.

The Love of the Heart of Jesus towards the Souls in Purgatory.

WE all hope one day that God, of His infinite mercy, will permit us to purify our unworthiness in these burning flames. There are souls to whom the love of the Heart of Jesus, in instituting this place of purification, is an almost overwhelming thought. It is a solemn joy, when we feel weighed down with the burden of our sins and unworthiness, to know, or at least to hope, that one day we shall be purified, and cleansed, and refined as the brightest gold. Every revelation on this subject, which has the sanction of the Church, must be a matter of the deepest interest to each individual. The revelations with which St. Gertrude was favoured on this subject, are of peculiar interest. They teach us most plainly the faults for which we are most likely to suffer, and hence we may learn what we should avoid,

and they show us the deep tenderness of the
Heart of Jesus Christ towards our suffering
brethren ; thus assuring us how acceptable to
Him will be our efforts to assist those who cannot assist themselves.

The pain of sense and the pain of love, strive
for the mastery in this region of pain and
love ; but the agony of sensible pain seems
almost overpowered by the keen, surpassing,
subduing, all-absorbing longing of the soul for
God. It pines for Him with a pining as far
beyond our words to tell, as it is beyond our
thoughts to conceive ; but it is held back by a
punishment proportioned and acutely corres-
ponding to the sin which had hindered it from
perfect union with God on earth.

Happy shall we be, if careful meditation on
those marvellous revelations, leads us to an
earnest strife against our besetting sin, and to
more constant and generous efforts to assist our
suffering brethren.

CHAPTER I.

OF THE LOVE OF THE HEART OF JESUS IN PURIFYING THE SOUL IN SICKNESS.

TWELVE days after the death of St. Gertrude, one of her spiritual daughters was also called to her eternal reward. Her death added much to the affliction of the religious, for her innocence and purity of heart had made her singularly beloved. As the favoured religious wept and prayed for her, and thought of how much her sisters had been deprived in losing her good example and her wise counsels, she ventured to exclaim: " Ah, my beloved Lord! why have You taken her so suddenly from us?" Our Lord replied: " While you were burying Gertrude, My beloved, I was taking My delight amongst your devoted community, where I had descended to feed upon the lilies; and as I beheld this lily, which pleased Me exceedingly, I took it in My hand; and as I held it therein for eleven days, before breaking it from the stem, it increased marvellously in beauty and in the odour of sanctity;

and then I took it to Myself for My own special delight." He then added : " When any of you reflect on the pleasures you found in her society, and desire to enjoy it again, if you offer this desire to Me, it renews the pleasure I find in the fragrance of this lily, and I will return it a hundredfold."

As the religious, like a faithful and loving sister, offered the Host at the Elevation for her soul, with all the fidelity of the Heart of Jesus, she saw her elevated to a higher and yet more sublime degree of glory, where her garments shone marvellously, and she was honoured by blessed spirits. And this she beheld whenever she made this offering for her.

Then, as she inquired of our Divine Lord, why the sister had appeared in great fear and alarm during her agony, she received this reply : " It was for her good, and an effect of My mercy. For during her sickness, she desired very much to be assisted by your prayers, so that she might be admitted into heaven immediately. I promised you this favour, which she believed she would obtain from Me. I was pleased with her confidence, and determined to do her yet more good than I had before purposed. But as young persons seldom purify themselves from slight negligences—such as seeking too much amusement, and taking pleasure in what is useless—and as it was necessary that she should be purified from these little stains by the inconveniences and pains of sickness, before I could bring her to heaven, I could not bear that, after having endured all with so much resignation and patience, she should still be unable to enjoy this blessedness. I therefore permitted her to be further tried by fear, caused by the sight of evil spirits, and thus she became perfectly purified, and merited eternal glory."   "But where wert Thou, then, O Lord?" inquired the religious. Our Lord replied: "I was hidden on her left side; and as soon as she was sufficiently purified, I showed Myself to her, and took her with Me to eternal rest and glory."

Another religious died soon after, who from her infancy had been specially devoted to the Mother of God. After she had received the last Sacraments, and when she appeared almost dead, she gave singular edification to the religious, by the affection and compunction with which she kissed the wounds of a crucifix which was presented to her, addressing it in the tenderest words. After pouring forth the most ardent and fervent ejaculations for pardon of her sins, for the protection of her Spouse in her last moments, and for the assistance of the Blessed Virgin, the angels and saints, her strength failed, and she passed, as in a quiet sleep, to her eternal reward. As the community were reciting the usual prayers for the repose of her soul, our Lord appeared to a religious with the deceased in His arms, saying to her caressingly, "Do you know Me, My child?" Then she, who was favoured with this vision, prayed that our Lord would specially reward that soul for her humble and efficacious charity in having served her on many occasions, and for having been specially earnest in doing service to those religious who were the most holy and devoted to God, in order that she might share in their merits and graces. Our Lord therefore presented His deified Heart to her, saying : "Drink freely from Me a reward for all which thou didst when on earth for My elect."

On the following day, at Mass, the soul appeared as if seated in our Lord's bosom, and His Blessed Mother appeared to rejoice this soul by a communication of her merits. This was specially the case while the community recited the Psalter for her, with the *Ave Maria;* so that, at each word the Mother of our Lord appeared to make presents to this soul, who received them to increase her merit before God. While they prayed thus, the religious desired much to know what faults the deceased had committed, from which it had been necessary to purify her before her death; and she prayed God to make this known to her. As her prayer was the result of a Divine inspiration, and not of an idle curiosity, it was heard, and our Lord replied : " She took some complacence in her own judgment; but I purified her from this, by causing her to die before the community had finished the prayers which they were offering for her. This troubled her much, because she feared it would prove an obstacle to her happiness, by depriving her of the assistance which she hoped to derive from the prayers of others."

To this the religious replied : " Lord, could she not have been purified from this by the sentiments of compunction which she had in imploring pardon for all her sins at the last moment of her life ?" Our Lord replied : " This general contrition was not sufficient, because she still had some confidence in her own judgment, and was not perfectly docile to those who instructed her ; and therefore it was necessary that she should be purified by this suffering." He added: " She also needed purification, for having sometimes neglected the grace of confession ; but My goodness remitted this fault to her for the sake of some persons whom I honour with My friendship, and of others who had charge of her, and for the pain and mortification I caused her by obliging her to confess, against her inclination, on the day of her death ; and then I pardoned her all the omissions she had been guilty of in this matter."

CHAPTER II.

HOW A DISOBEDIENCE WAS EXPIATED BY AN ILLNESS.

S Gertrude recited five *Pater nosters* for Dame S.—the eldest of the community, who had received Extreme Unction, and at last ended her prayer in the Wound of our Lord's Side—she besought Him to purify this soul with the water which flowed therefrom, and to adorn it with the merits of His most precious Blood. She then saw this soul, under the form of a young virgin, crowned with a golden circlet, and supported by our Divine Lord, who imparted the graces she had asked to her soul. She understood by this, that the sister must remain longer on earth, to be purified from a disobedience of which she had been guilty, in conversing* more than was right with a sick person: and this was accomplished. She suffered for five months in a manner which sufficiently manifested the fault from which she was being purified. On the day on which she was taken ill, she appeared very joyful, as if our Lord had granted her some great favour, and she attempted to relate what had happened to her ; but as she had not the perfect use of her senses, she was unable to do so.   But as she saw Gertrude standing by her, with some of the other religious, she called her by name, and said : " Do you speak for me, for you know all."   St. Gertrude began to relate what had been revealed to her, and the invalid was then able to continue the recital herself.   When the others made any observation, she at once refuted their assertions, declaring that our Lord had forgiven her sins, and bestowed many favours on her.

* " Communicans."

On the day before her death, St. Gertrude beheld our Lord preparing a place for her in His Divine arms; but the soul appeared at His left, and separated from Him by a little cloud. She then said: "Lord, this place which Thou hast prepared will not be suitable for a soul covered with this cloud." He replied: " She will remain a little longer on earth, that she may become fit for it." And it was even so; for the religious continued all that day and the following night in her agony. Next morning she beheld our Lord coming towards the dying nun with marks of the greatest tenderness; and she appeared to rise, as if to meet Him. Then St. Gertrude said: "Art Thou not come now to take this desolate soul to Thyself, as a merciful Father?" and our Lord indicated by a sign that He had this intention.

Soon after her decease, she saw this soul again, under the form of a young virgin, adorned with roses, and advancing joyfully to her Spouse; but when she came near him, she fell at His feet as if almost deprived of life, until the words *Tibi supplicatio commendet Ecclesiæ* were repeated, when she arose, and cast herself into the Divine arms, where she is eternally replenished with the treasures of beatitude.

CHAPTER III.

HOW THE SOUL DESIRES TO BE PURIFIED AFTER DEATH.

TWO ladies, more illustrious for their virtue than their distinguished birth — sisters in the flesh, but yet more closely united in the spirit by their equality in perfection—were called to the heavenly nuptials by their celestial Spouse, after having lived a most holy life from their very childhood. The first died on the glorious Feast of the Assumption, which was also the day of her profession; the other sister died thirty days after; but their deaths were so edifying and blessed, that we are about to relate some circumstances concerning them. .

As Gertrude prayed for the eldest, who died on the Assumption, she appeared to her, surrounded with a glorious light, and magnificently adorned, standing before the throne of Jesus Christ; but she seemed ashamed to lift up her eyes to Him, or to gaze upon His majestic countenance. When the Saint perceived this, she was moved to pity, and said to our Lord : " Alas ! most loving Lord, why dost Thou permit her to stand before Thee as a stranger, without manifesting any tokens of affection for her ?" Our Lord then extended His hand to her, as if to draw her to Himself; but she drew back from Him with reverent fear.

As Gertrude marvelled much at this, she said to the soul : " Why do you thus fly from the embraces of your Spouse ?" She replied : " Because I am not yet perfectly purified from my defects, and am not in a condition to receive His favours. Even if Divine justice did not restrain me, I would deprive myself of these favours, of which I am not worthy." Gertrude then said : " How can this be, when I now see you standing before God in such glory ?" The soul answered : " Although all creatures are present to God, yet souls come near Him in proportion to their perfection in charity ; but none are worthy of this blessedness who are not perfectly purified from all the stains which they have contracted during their mortal lives."

A month after, when the second sister was in her agony, St. Gertrude prayed for her very earnestly. After her death, she appeared to her, surrounded with light, as a young virgin, clothed in a purple robe, that she might be presented to her Spouse. She also saw Jesus Christ, who stood near her, and who caused a certain consolation to proceed from His Wounds, to refresh and strengthen her five senses, so that the soul was exceedingly consoled thereby. St. Gertrude then said to our Lord : "Since Thou art the God of all consolation, why dost Thou permit this soul to appear so sad, as if troubled by some secret grief ?" He answered : "I now manifest to her My Humanity, which does not perfectly console her ; for thus I reward the special love which she manifested for My Passion in the last moments of her life. But when she is perfectly freed from all her stains, I will manifest the joys of My Divinity to her, and then she will have all she desires." "But, Lord," continued the Saint, "how is it that all her faults were not perfectly purified by the charity which she possessed at the last moment of her life, since Scripture teaches that man shall be judged according to the state in which he dies ?"

The Lord answered : "When a man loses his strength, he has no longer the power to execute his good designs, though he may have the will to do so. When, of My gratuitous goodness, I inspire these desires, and give this will, I do

not always efface thereby the stains of past negligences, which would no doubt be accomplished
if the person recovered health and strength, and
then began to reform his life thoroughly." She
replied: "Alas, Lord! cannot Thy abundant
mercy remit the sins of this soul, who has loved
Thee so ardently from her very childhood?" He
answered: "I will indeed reward her love
abundantly; but My justice must first be satisfied by the removal of her stains." Our Lord
then turned lovingly to this soul, and said to
her: "My spouse will consent willingly to what
My justice requires; and when she is purified,
she will enjoy My glory and consolation." As
she consented, our Lord seemed to ascend into
heaven, and to leave her after Him where she
was; but she appeared as if ardently desiring to
follow Him. The solitude was to purify her
from the stains which she had contracted by
conversing too freely with the other sex; and
the efforts she made to ascend upwards purified
her from some faults of indolence.

On another occasion, as St. Gertrude prayed
for the same person at Mass, she said, at the
Elevation of the Host: "Holy Father, I offer
this Host to Thee for this soul on the part of
all in heaven, on earth, and in the deep;" and

she beheld this soul in the air, surrounded by a multitude of persons, who held representations of the Host in their hands, which they offered up on bended knees. The soul appeared to receive great assistance and inestimable joy from this devotion. Then the soul said: " I now experience the truth of what is said in Scripture, that no good action, however trifling, will fail to be rewarded ; and that no negligence, however trifling, will be unpunished ; for this offering of the Sacrament of the altar procures the greatest consolation for me, on account of my former devotion in receiving It ; and the ardent charity which I had for others greatly enhances the prayers which are made for me ; while for both of these things I shall receive an eternal recompense."

The soul then appeared as if elevated higher and higher by the prayers of the Church ; and when her purification was accomplished, the Saint beheld our Lord coming for her, to crown her as a queen, and to conduct her to eternal joys.

CHAPTER IV.

OF THE AGONY AND DEATH OF M. B., AND OF
HER BLESSED SOUL—HOW SALUTARY IT IS
TO ASSIST THE SOULS IN PURGATORY.

WHEN M. B., of happy memory, was in
her agony, Gertrude prayed for her
most earnestly, and obtained a knowledge of what was passing around her in this last
combat.   For a whole hour she beheld nothing
but the trouble which the soul endured for having sometimes taken undue pleasure in exterior
things ; such as, for having had a coverlet of
coloured cloth on her bed, embroidered with
gold.*   On the day of her decease, when Mass
was celebrated, Gertrude offered the Host for
her ; although she did not see her, she knew
that she was present, and addressed our Lord

---

* "Quod lectus ipsius fuit depositus de picto panno,"
&c.   This, doubtless, was before the religious had
entered the monastery, as the rule of poverty of every
religious house would forbid such extravagance.   The
richly embroidered quilt was a very pitch of luxurious
refinement in that age, and hence indicated a habit of
self-indulgence or luxurious tastes, which probably
caused the soul's suffering for an act which was only its
climax.

thus, as if seeking her, saying : " O Lord, where
is she ?" He replied : "She will come to Me
pure and white." From this she understood
that the prayers which were offered in charity
had obtained great grace for her in her last
moments ; and that some persons, moved by
holy zeal, had offered their good works for her,
and charged themselves with the penalties due
to her.

As Gertrude prayed for her again at the Mass
which preceded her interment, she beheld her
seated at a festal table beside our Lord, where
the prayers which had been offered were given
to her under the form of different kinds of food.
At the Elevation, as the Saint offered the chalice
for her, our Lord appeared to present it to her
Himself. When she had tasted it, she immediately became penetrated with Divine sweetness,
and rose up to pray for all who had ever injured
her, either by thought, word, or act, rejoicing
for the merit which they had obtained for her
thereby. Then Gertrude inquired why she did
not pray for her friends also; but she replied: " I
pray for them more efficaciously by speaking
heart to heart to my Beloved."

On another occasion, as she remarked that
she had offered all her merits for the deceased,

she said to our Lord :* "I hope, O Lord, that Thou wilt frequently cast the eyes of Thy mercy on my indigence." He replied: "What can I do more for one who has thus deprived herself of all things through charity, than to cover her immediately with charity?" She answered: "Whatever Thou mayest do, I shall always appear before Thee destitute of all merit, for I have renounced all I have gained or may gain." He replied: "Do you not know that a mother would allow a child who was well clothed to sit at her feet, but she would take one who was barely clad into her arms, and cover her with her own garment?" He added: "And now, what advantage have you, who are seated on the shore of an ocean, over those who sit by a little rivulet?" That is to say, those who keep their good works for themselves have the rivulet; but those who renounce them in love and humility, possess God, who is an inexhaustible ocean of beatitude.

* The French translations have, "Elle resentit quelque espèce de tristesse,"—a sentiment utterly un- worthy of so generous and noble a soul, who could not regret what she had so freely and lovingly bestowed; but it is not in any Latin edition which we have seen.

CHAPTER V.

HOW THE SOULS OF G. AND B. WERE PURIFIED FOR NEGLECTING CONFESSION, AND FOR TAKING PLEASURE IN EARTHLY THINGS.

AS Scripture testifies that "By what things a man sinneth, by the same also he is punished" (Wis. ii. 17), and, on the contrary, that he will be rewarded in the things in which he has suffered or done good, we give the following examples for the benefit of our readers.

We had two persons with us, who were both ill at the same time; one evidently suffered from a severe affection of the chest, and hence she was attended more carefully. The other, whose disease was not known, and who seemed more likely to live, did not receive so much care; but, as men are often deceived, the one for whom we feared the least died the first, and the other survived a month longer. When the former approached her end, she had been strengthened in grace by great patience and devotion, which had purified her soul exceedingly ; for the ardent love which our Lord had for His spouse would not suffer Him to permit the least stain to remain on her. Nevertheless, she still needed some purification for having too easily omitted confession ; for sometimes, when the priest came to her, she feigned to be sleeping, not having any grave fault to accuse herself of. As the hour approached when she was to be received to the eternal embraces of her Spouse, He purified her from this stain. For, when she asked for a confessor, she lost the power of speech when he came, and then she feared exceedingly that she would suffer for her former negligence after death ; and so was purified from her fault by this excessive fear.

Thus, being entirely purified and freed from every stain, she was released from the prison of the flesh, and received into eternal glory. Many revelations concerning this were made to Gertrude.

One of these was, that when she was brought to our Lord's throne of glory, He conferred this privilege on her, of seeming to soothe her, as a mother would a child when she wished her to take some bitter medicine ; and He did this to console her for some little inattention which had been shown her, in consequence of the religious being so much occupied in attending to her companion, whom they believed to be dangerously ill.

Our Lord then said to her : " Tell Me, My daughter, what you would wish Me to do for the soul of your companion ; and what consolation you desire Me to give her." She replied : " Give her the same gifts Thou hast bestowed on me, my dearest Lord ; for I cannot imagine any more consoling." And our Lord promised to comply with her request.

The other religious died a month later. The day after her death she was seen marvellously adorned, as a reward for the exceeding innocence and simplicity of her life, and her exactness in observing all the austerities of her Order ; but she had one stain from which she needed purification, and this was having received unnecessary consolations in her illness. She was purified in this manner : She stood at the gate of a palace, where our Lord was seated on a throne of glory, with a countenance so full of sweetness and love, that no human intellect could describe His beauty. He appeared anxious to receive His spouse ; but when she attempted to approach, she found herself withheld by nails, which fastened her garments to the ground ; and these nails were the imperfections she had committed in her sickness. But Gertrude, who was touched with compassion, prayed for her, and our Lord freed her from this impediment. Then the Saint said to our Lord : "Why was this soul freed by my prayers, and not restored by the prayers of those who loved her so much, and who prayed for her with such fervour and affection ?" He replied : "Their prayers have been of great service to her ; but they did not remove the impediment which I have revealed to you, and from which she has been released by your prayers." She continued : "How hast Thou fulfilled Thy promise to treat this person with the same goodness as Thou didst manifest to her who died first ? for she has lived longer in religion, and seemed to abound more in virtue ; and yet the other appeared at once in Thy presence, and in greater glory." He answered : "My justice is immutable, for I reward each according to her works. She who has laboured least, cannot receive more than she who has laboured most, unless she has worked with a purer intention, a more fervent charity, or a more earnest strife ; but My mercy rewards works of supererogation, such as the prayers of the faithful ; and thus My rewards are not always proportioned to the person's actual merit."

Hence we may learn how carefully we should avoid taking pleasure in anything earthly, since this blessed soul was thus detained from happiness for this imperfection. This was even more fully manifested to St. Gertrude in another vision, in which she saw her before the throne of God, manifesting the same ardour as she had done at the gate; not, indeed, desiring to approach, but appearing as if unable to move—and this was the second obstacle to her happiness; and even when she was freed from this, her happiness was not perfectly complete, until our Lord placed a magnificent crown on her head, which He held in His hand, and which she received with exceeding joy.

As St. Gertrude beheld this, she said to our Lord : " Why has this soul been tormented so painfully, where Thou art all-powerful ?" He replied : " She has not been tormented, but has waited with joy for the consummation of her happiness; even as a young girl would wait for a festival on which she was to be adorned with the ornaments which her mother had prepared for her."

After this the soul thanked the Saint for the

prayers which she had offered for her ; and Gertrude said to her : "Why did you not receive willingly some admonition which I gave you during your sickness, although you always seemed so much attached to me?" The soul replied : "It is for this reason that your prayers have now more power with God, since they are offered more purely out of charity."

CHAPTER VI.

THOSE WHO HAVE PERSEVERED LONG IN SIN ARE NOT EASILY BENEFITED BY THE PRAYERS OF THE CHURCH, AND ARE LIBERATED WITH DIFFICULTY.

ONCE, when a person was told that a relative had died, of whose state she had great fear, Gertrude was so moved by her affliction, that she offered to pray for the soul of the deceased. Our Lord taught her, that the information had been given in her presence by a special arrangement of His providence. She replied : "Lord, couldst not Thou have given me the compassion without this?" He answered: " I take particular pleasure in prayers for the dead, when they are addressed to Me from natural compassion, united to a good-will; thus a good work becomes perfected."

When Gertrude had prayed for this soul a long time, he appeared to her under a horrible form, as if blackened by fire, and contorted with pain. She saw no one near him; but his sins, which he had not fully expiated, were his executioners, and each member suffered for the sins to which it had been accessory. Then St. Gertrude, desiring to intercede with her Spouse for him, said lovingly: "My Lord, wilt Thou not relieve this soul, for my sake?" He replied: "Not only would I deliver this soul, but thousands of souls, for your love! How do you wish Me to show him mercy?—shall I release him at once from all his pains?" "Perhaps, Lord," she continued, "this would be contrary to the decrees of Thy justice." He answered: "It would not be contrary to it if you asked me with faith; for, as I foresee the future, I prepared him for this when in his agony." She replied: "I beseech of Thee, Salvation of my soul, to perfect this work according to Thy mercy, in which I have the most perfect confidence."

When she had said this, the soul appeared under

human form and in great joy, but still bearing
some marks of his former sins ; however, the
Saint knew that he must be purified further, and
made as white as snow, before he would be fit
to enter into the Divine presence ; and to effect
this, it was necessary for him to suffer as if from
the blows of an iron hammer ; furthermore, he
had continued so long in sin, that the process of
cleansing his soul was much prolonged, and he
also suffered as if exposed for a year to the rays
of a scorching sun. As the saint marvelled at
this, she was instructed that those who have
committed many and grievous sins are not assisted by the ordinary suffrages of the Church,
until they are partly purified by Divine justice ;
and that they cannot avail themselves of the
prayers of the faithful, which are constantly
descending on the souls in purgatory, like a gentle
and refreshing dew, or like a sweet and soothing
ointment.

Gertrude then returned thanks for this favour,
and said to the Lord : " O my most loving Lord,
tell me, I beseech Thee, what work or prayers
will most easily obtain mercy from Thee,
for those sinners who have died in a state
of grace, so that they may be delivered from
this terrible impediment which prevents them

from obtaining the benefit of the Church's prayers? For this soul appears to me now, when relieved from this burden, as if it had ascended from hell to heaven." Our Lord replied: "The only way to obtain such a favour is Divine love; neither prayers nor any other labours will avail without this, and it must be such a love as you now have for Me; and as none can have this grace unless I bestow it, so also none can obtain these advantages after death unless I have prepared them for it by some special grace during life. Know, however, that the prayers and labours of the faithful relieve the soul gradually from this heavy burden, and that they are delivered sooner or later, according to the fervour and pure intentions of those who thus serve them, and according to the merit which they have acquired for themselves when in this life."

Then the soul besought our Lord, by the love which had brought Him down from heaven to die upon the cross, that He would apply these remedies to his soul, and reward those who prayed for him abundantly; and our Lord appeared to take a piece of gold from him, and lay it by to recompense those who had assisted him by their prayers.

CHAPTER VII.

OF PRAYERS FOR THE SOULS OF DECEASED PARENTS.

N the Sunday on which the community prayed for the souls of deceased parents,* as St. Gertrude offered the Host, after she had received Holy Communion, for the repose of their souls, she beheld an immense number coming forth from a place of darkness like sparks of fire; some in the form of stars, and others in other shapes. Then she inquired if this great multitude could be all composed of the souls of the deceased parents; and our Lord replied : " I am your nearest

* In all conventual houses, the parents of each religious are considered the special charge of all. Mass, Communion, and the Office of the Dead are regularly offered for all deceased parents, at stated periods throughout the year. Alas ! what do not those unhappy persons lose, both in time and in eternity, who hinder the consecration of their children to God ! and what gain is theirs, who, by placing them in a holy and devoted community, secure the prayers of the most saintly souls for their own welfare, both in this world and the next! Perhaps only those who are inmates of the cloister know with what tender and fervent affection the relations of each member are prayed for by all.

Relation,* your Father, your Brother, and your Spouse; therefore, My special friends are also yours, and I could not exclude them from the commemoration of your parents; therefore, you behold them all united together." From henceforward the Saint prayed constantly for those who were specially beloved by our Lord. On the following day, at Mass, after the Elevation, she heard our Lord saying: "We have eaten with those who came and were ready; we must now send to those who could not come to the feast." Another year, when the bell tolled for the Office of the Dead, she beheld a snow-white lamb, such as the paschal lamb is usually painted; and, from a wound in its heart, a stream of blood flowed into a chalice, while it said: "I will now be a propitiation for those souls for whom a feast is prepared here to-day."

* "Ego propinquissimus vester sum."

PART V.

PART V.

Revelations of the Love of the Heart of Jesus to His Mother.

WE cannot separate devotion to Mary from devotion to Jesus. Hence the Saints who have loved Jesus must have also loved Mary with a more than ordinary devotion. This devotion to Mary is the stumbling-block of heresy; and we should rather have expected than be surprised that it is so. The Church has especially distinguished the Mother of God as the sole destroyer of heresies.

Can we then marvel if the author of heresy should view the devotion to her with the utmost alarm, and strive with unwearied energy and will to turn his unhappy victims from Mary?

It is simply because the doctrine of the Incarnation is not, and cannot be, fully understood outside the Church, that devotion to Mary is opposed and misrepresented. Those who do not deny the love of a St. Bernard or a St. Liguori for Jesus, are fain to explain away, if not to be much scandalized, at their love of Mary. Those who believe that in the Most Holy Sacrament they receive the Flesh of the Son of God, and who believe also that He took Flesh in Mary's womb, cannot marvel that the tree which bore this Fruit, which nourished It in no mystic manner, but as the ordinary human life of a child is nourished by a mother with her blood and her milk, they cannot wonder that those who love an Incarnate God most ardently, must love also most ardently the Mother of whom He took Flesh.

Our Saint is no exception to the ordinary rule of loving Mary much, because of loving Jesus much. Her revelations are teeming with thoughts of Mary, with prayers to her, with praises of her exalted privileges. Jesus Himself, who inspires the souls most dear to Him with the devotion most dear to the Heart of a Son, the love of His Mother, reveals to His beloved one the glories of her whom He delights to honour, and imparts the gift of devotion to Mary to this favoured soul, not as a gift which she must use sparingly and cautiously, but as one of the greatest helps to the attainment of more than ordinary sanctity.

CHAPTER I.

HOW THE HEART OF JESUS DESIRES THAT HIS MOTHER SHOULD BE HONOURED.

AS Gertrude offered herself to God during her prayer, and inquired how He desired her to occupy herself at this time, He replied : " Honour My Mother, who is seated at My side, and employ yourself in praising her." Then the Saint began to salute the Queen of heaven, reciting the verse, *Paradisus voluptas*, &c.—" Paradise of delights ;" and extolling her because she was the abode full of delights which the impenetrable wisdom of God, who knows all creatures perfectly, had chosen for His dwelling ; and she besought her to obtain for her a heart adorned with so many virtues, that God might take pleasure in dwelling therein. Then the Blessed Virgin inclined towards her, and planted in her heart the different flowers of virtue—the rose of charity, the lily of chastity, the violet of humility, the flexibility of obedience, and many other gifts ; thus showing how promptly she assists those who invoke her assistance.

Then the Saint addressed her thus: *Gaude, morum disciplina*—" Rejoice, model of discipline ;" praising her for having ordered her desires, judgment, and affection with more care and circumspection than the rest of mankind, and for having served the Lord, who dwelt in her, with such respect and reverence, that she had never given Him the least occasion or pain in her thoughts, words, or actions. Having besought her to obtain for her also the same grace, it appeared to her that the Mother of God sent her all her affections under the form of young virgins, recommending each in particular to unite her dispositions to those of her client, and to supply for any defects into which she might fall. By this also she understood with what promptitude the Blessed Virgin assists those who invoke her. Then the Saint besought our Lord to supply for her omissions in devotion to His Blessed Mother, which He was pleased to do.

The following day, as Gertrude prayed, the Mother of God appeared to her, in the presence of the ever-adorable Trinity, under the form of a white lily, with three leaves; one standing erect, and the other two bent down. By this she understood that it was not without reason that the Blessed Mother of God was called the white lily of the Trinity, since she contained in herself, with more plenitude and perfection than any other creature, the virtues of the Most Holy Trinity, which she had never sullied by the slightest stain of sin. The upright leaf of the lily represented the omnipotence of God the Father, and the two leaves which bent down the wisdom and love of the Son and the Holy Spirit, to which the Holy Virgin approaches so nearly. Then the Blessed Virgin made known to her that if any one salutes her devoutly as the white lily of the Trinity and the vermilion rose of heaven, she will show her how she prevails by the omnipotence of the Father, how skilful she is in procuring the salvation of men by the wisdom of the Son, and with what an exceeding love her heart is filled by the charity of the Holy Ghost. The Blessed Virgin added these words: "I will appear at the hour of death to those who salute me thus in such glory, that they will anticipate the very joys of heaven." From this time the Saint frequently saluted the Holy Virgin or her images with these words: "Hail, white lily of the ever-peaceful and glorious Trinity! hail, effulgent rose, the delight of heaven, of whom the King of heaven was born, and by whose milk He was nourished! do thou feed our souls by the effusions of thy Divine influences."

CHAPTER II.

HOW POWERFULLY THE BLESSED VIRGIN PRO-
TECTS THOSE WHO INVOKE HER; AND HOW
WE MAY SUPPLY FOR OUR NEGLIGENCES IN
HER SERVICE.

ON the glorious Feast of the Nativity of the Blessed Virgin, St. Gertrude, having said as many *Ave Marias* as she had remained days in her mother's womb, offered them to her devoutly, and inquired what merit they would have who performed a like devotion. This benign Virgin replied: "They will merit a special share in the joys which I possess in heaven, which are continually renewed, and in the virtues with which the ever-blessed and glorious Trinity adorns me."

At the Antiphon *Ave decus*, she beheld the heavens opening, while the angels descended and placed a magnificent throne in the centre of the choir, whereon the Queen of glory was seated, and manifested how lovingly she received the prayers and devotion of the religious on this Festival. The angels stood round this throne, attending the Mother of their God with the greatest respect and joy. The Saint also saw an angel standing by each of the religious, with a branch in his hand; and this branch produced different kinds of fruit and flowers, according to the devotion of the sister who was thus attended. At the conclusion of the Office, the angels brought these branches to the Blessed Virgin to adorn her throne. Then Gertrude exclaimed: "Alas, kind Mother! I do not deserve to be thus united with the choirs of the blessed." She replied: "Your good-will suffices; and the devout intention which you had at Vespers, of offering your prayers through the sweet Heart of my Son, in my honour, far exceeds any corporal work; to assure you of this, I will present your branch of fruit and flowers to the adorable Trinity, as an oblation of the highest merit."

At Matins she beheld how the angels gathered the flowers and fruit of the different intentions of the religious, and presented them to the Virgin Mother. The flowers appeared more brilliant and beautiful in proportion to the earnestness of each; and the sweetness of the fruit corresponded with the purity and fervour of their devotion.

At the *Gloria Patri* of the fourth Response,* as St. Gertrude praised the ineffable power of the Father, the incomprehensible wisdom of the Son, and the marvellous benignity of the Holy Ghost, in having given us a creature so full of grace to further our salvation, the Blessed Virgin stood before the Blessed Trinity, praying that the Divine Omnipotence, Wisdom, and Goodness would bestow as much grace on St. Gertrude as it was possible for any creature to receive ; and the Blessed Trinity poured forth an abundant benediction of grace upon her soul, which watered it like a gentle rain.

Then St. Gertrude chanted the Antiphon *Quam pulchra es*, in the person of the Son of God, in honour of His Father. This was accepted with great love by our Lord, who said to her: " I will reward you at a fitting time, according to My royal munificence, for the honour you have paid to my beloved Mother."†

---

* It will be remembered that there are four Lessons in each Nocturn of the Benedictine Office. The *Gloria Patri* is said at the end of the fourth Response of each Nocturn.

† "Dulcissimæ genetrici."

At the Antiphon *Adest*, when the words *Ipsa intercedat pro peccatis nostris* were chanted, she saw the Blessed Virgin with a parchment in her hand, on which the words, "She will intercede," were written in letters of gold; and this she presented to her Son by the ministry of angels. He replied lovingly : "I give thee full power, by My omnipotence, to be propitious to all who invoke thy aid, in whatever manner is most pleasing to thee."

As the Sequence *Ave præclara** was chanted at Mass, at the words *Ora Virgo nos*, the Blessed Virgin turned towards her Son, and prayed for the community with her hands clasped. Then our Lord turned towards them, and blessed them with the sign of the cross, to prepare them to receive the adorable Sacrament of His Body and Blood.

At the words *Audi nos*, the Blessed Virgin appeared seated on a high throne with her Divine Son ; and St. Gertrude addressed her thus : "Why do you not pray for us, O Mother of mercy ?" She replied : " I speak for you to my Beloved, heart to heart." Then, when the same words were repeated again, the Virgin extended

---

* We have not been able to verify this Sequence.

her royal hands over the convent, as if uniting herself to their desires, and praying as one with them to her Divine Son ; and this royal Son, at the following verse, *Salve nos, Jesu*, turning towards the community, said to them : "I am ready to accomplish all your desires."

Then, as St. Gertrude reflected on the approaching Festival, and ardently desired that her heart might be prepared to solemnise it, she said to the Mother of God : " Since the glory of your Assumption moves the souls of those who meditate on it so deeply, I desire much to know what the angels think of the Feast of your Nativity in heaven, that our devotion may be increased thereby on earth." The Blessed Virgin replied: " The angels commemorate the ineffable joys which I experienced while in the womb of my Mother, when they offer me their homage with the deepest reverence. The archangels also contemplate, in the mirror of the Blessed Trinity, the eminent favours and graces which God bestowed on me above all creatures, and minister to me also ; while all the heavenly orders unite in serving and assisting me, for the glory of God ; and for this they are now recompensed with special joys."

At Compline, as the *Salve Regina** was chanted, St. Gertrude grieved before God that she had never served His Mother with the veneration due to her; and she offered this Antiphon, through the Heart of Jesus, to supply for her defects; and our Lord supplied -for her deficiencies by little tubes of gold, which passed from His Heart to the heart of His Virgin Mother, and through which He poured forth on her the tenderness of His filial affection. We may also supply for our negligences by the following prayer, or any similar one :

"O sweetest Jesus, I beseech Thee, by the love which caused Thee to take flesh in the bosom of this most pure Virgin, that Thou wouldst supply for our defects in the service and honour of this most benign Mother, who is ever ready to assist us, with maternal tenderness, in all our necessities. Offer her, O sweetest Jesus, the superabundant beautitude of Thy sweetest

---

* Anthem at Vespers from Trinity Sunday until Advent. It is generally believed that Adelmar, Bishop of Puy, composed this most touching devotion; the last words, "O clement," &c., were added by St. Bernard. Adelmar lived in the eleventh century, and the *Salve Regina* was introduced about that time into the services of the Church. Some authors attribute it to Hermann Contractus, a Benedictine monk of the same date.

Heart; show her Thy Divine predilection, which chose her from all eternity, before all creatures, to be Thy Mother, adorning her with every grace and virtue; remind her of all the tenderness Thou didst manifest to her when on earth, Thy filial obedience to her in all things, and, above all, Thy care at the hour of Thy Death, when Thou didst forget Thine own anguish to solace hers, and didst provide her with a son; remind her, also, of the joys and glory of her Assumption, when she was exalted above all the choirs of angels, and constituted Queen of heaven and earth. Thus, O good Jesus, do Thou make Thy Mother propitious to us, that she may be our advocate and protector in life and in death."

At the *Eia ergo*, as St. Gertrude invoked this most benign Mother, she saw her inclining towards her, as if drawn by cords; by which she understood, that when we invoke her devoutly as our *advocate*, her maternal tenderness is so moved, that she cannot fail to assist us. At the words *Illos tuos misericordes oculos*, the Blessed Virgin inclined the eyes of her Son towards the earth, saying: "These are my merciful eyes, which I incline towards all who invoke me devoutly, and from them they obtain the fruit of eternal salvation." Then the Saint was taught by our Lord to salute His Blessed Mother, at least daily, by the words *Eia ergo*, and *Advocata nostra*, assuring her that she would obtain great consolation thereby at the hour of her death.

St. Gertrude then offered our Lady a hundred and fifty *Ave Marias*, beseeching her to assist her at the hour of death by her maternal tenderness; and each word she repeated appeared like a piece of gold, which our Lord offered to His Mother, who used them for the help and consolation of the Saint at the hour of her death. Thus she knew that when we recommend our end to any Saint, the prayers which are offered to them are presented before the tribunal of the Judge, and the Saint to whom we have recommended ourselves is appointed our advocate.

CHAPTER III.

HOW WE MAY REMEMBER THE PASSION OF
CHRIST, AND PROCLAIM THE PRAISES OF THE
VIRGIN MOTHER OF GOD, IN RECITING THE
SEVEN CANONICAL HOURS.

ONE night, as Gertrude kept vigil, and
was occupied with the remembrance of
the Lord's Passion, as she felt much
fatigued, although she had not yet recited
Matins, she said to God : " Ah, my Lord, since
Thou knowest that my weakness requires rest,
teach me what honour and what service I can
render to Thy Blessed Mother, now that it is
not in my power to recite her Office."* "Glorify
Me," replied our Lord, " through My loving
Heart, for the innocence of that spotless virginity
by which she conceived Me, being a virgin ;
brought Me forth, being a virgin ; and still remained a pure and spotless virgin after childbirth ; imitating thus My innocence when I was

---

* Not of obligation, but recited by some religious who
are not bound to recite the Divine Office, and also by
several of the contemplative orders, as a matter of devotion, after they have recited their Office of obligation.

taken at the hour of Matins for the redemption
of the human race, and was bound, struck with
rods, buffeted, and overwhelmed pitilessly with
every kind of misery and opprobrium." While
she did this, it appeared to her that the Lord
presented His Divine Heart to the most holy
Virgin His Mother, under the figure of a golden
cup, that she might drink from it ; and that,
being satiated with this sweet beverage—or
rather abundantly inebriated thereby—her very
soul might be filled with exceeding gladness.

Then Gertrude praised the Blessed Virgin,
saying to her : "I salute thee, most Blessed
Mother, august Sanctuary of the Holy Spirit,
through the sweetest Heart of Jesus Christ, thy
beloved Son and the Son of the Eternal Father,
beseeching thee to assist us in all our necessities,
both now and in the hour of our death. Amen."
She knew, when any one glorified our Lord in
these words, and added, in praise of the Blessed
Virgin, "I praise and salute thee, O Mother,"
&c., that each time He presented her His Divine
Heart to satisfy her thirst in the manner above
described, it gave exceeding satisfaction to the
Queen of Virgins to be saluted thus ; and that
she would recompense it according to the extent
of her liberality and maternal tenderness.

Our Lord then added : " At the hour of·
Prime, praise Me, through My sweetest ·Heart,
for the most peaceful humility with which the
Immaculate Virgin disposed herself more and
more to receive Me, and imitated the humility
with which I, who am the judge of the living
and the dead, willed at the same hour to submit
Myself to a Gentile, to be judged by ·him for
the redemption of mankind.

" At Tierce, praise Me for the fervent desires
by which the Blessed Virgin drew Me down
into her virginal womb from the bosom of My
Eternal Father, and imitated Me in the ardour
and zeal with which I desired the salvation of
men, when, being torn with whips, and crowned
with thorns, I bore, at the third hour, a shame-
ful and infamous cross on My shoulders with
extreme meekness and patience.

" At Sext, praise Me for the firm and assured
hope with ·which this celestial Virgin thought
only of glorifying Me by the purity of her intentions ; in which she imitated Me when I,·
being suspended on the tree of the cross, in all
the bitterness and anguish of death, longed with
My whole soul for the redemption of the human
race, crying out, ' I thirst !'—that is, for the
salvation of men ; so that, had it been necessary▸

for Me to suffer more bitter or cruel torments, I would willingly have borne them for their redemption.

"At None, praise Me for the ardent and mutual love which united My Divine Heart to that of the spotless Virgin, and which united and inseparably conjoined My all-glorious Divinity with My Humanity in her chaste womb, imitating Me in My mortal life until I expired on the cross at the ninth hour for the salvation of men.

"At Vespers, praise Me for the constant faith of My Blessed Mother at My death, during the desertion of My Apostles, and the despair of all; in which she imitated the fidelity with which I descended into limbo after My death, that I might withdraw those souls by My all-powerful hand and mercy, and bring them to the joys of paradise.

"At Compline, praise Me for the incomparable perseverance with which My sweetest Mother persevered in every virtue even to the end, and imitated Me in the work of man's redemption, which I accomplished with so much care, that after I had obtained their perfect redemption by a most cruel death, I nevertheless allowed My incorruptible Body to be laid in the tomb, to show that there is no degree of contempt or humiliation to which I would not submit for the welfare of man."

CHAPTER IV.

HOW GERTRUDE WAS TAUGHT BY THE HEART OF JESUS TO HONOUR HIS BLESSED MOTHER ON THE FEAST OF HIS NATIVITY.

AS the Saint was watching during the greater part of the night which preceded the vigil of Christmas, before Matins, and had occupied herself entirely in meditating on the Response *De illa occulta*, in which she took great pleasure, she was suddenly ravished in spirit, and in her rapture she beheld Jesus Christ reposing sweetly and peacefully in the bosom of His Father ; and the desires which were addressed to Him by those who wished to spend this feast with great devotion, appeared under the figure of a certain vapour. Then this beautiful and gentle Jesus sent forth from His Divine Heart a light which spread itself over this vapour, which showed them the way in which they should come to Him. As each approached to God, she perceived that those who had recommended themselves humbly to the prayers of others were led by the hand by persons who surrounded them, and thus they went direct to God in the splendour of this light, which came forth from His Heart; whereas those who had confided merely in their own efforts and prayers wandered from this path, but arrived at last at the termination by a light which came to them from God.

As the Saint desired to know with what special grace it had pleased God to communicate Himself to each of her sisters, she immediately beheld them all reposing in the bosom of the Son of God, where each was filled with joy according to her capacity and desires. She observed that none hindered the other, but that each enjoyed God as fully as if He had given Himself to each individually; that some embraced Him lovingly, as a Child about to be born for us; that others regarded Him as a faithful Friend, to whom they could therefore disclose every secret of their hearts; while others, pouring forth the whole joy of their souls, caressed Him as a Spouse chosen amongst a thousand, and more beloved than all—so that each found in Him, in a most pure and holy manner, the accomplishment of her individual desires.

Then the Saint came forward, according to her usual custom, and cast herself at the feet of her Lord, saying to Him: "O most loving Lord, what should my dispositions be, and what devotion can I offer to Thy most blessed Mother at this Divine birth, since my bodily infirmity prevents me even from reciting the Hours to which my profession obliges me ?" It appeared to her then that our Lord, moved by compassion for her poverty, gathered together all that she had said for the glory of God or the good of souls during the Advent, and offered it lovingly to His sweetest Mother, who was seated in glory at His side ; and to this He joined all the fruits which her words might have produced, even to the end of ages, to supply for any negligence which she might have committed in her service. The Mother of God, having received this offering, appeared as if adorned by it ; and Gertrude approached her, beseeching her to intercede for her with her Son. Then the Blessed Virgin turned towards Him with a loving countenance, and, after embracing Him, addressed Him thus : "My beloved Son, I beseech Thee to join Thy affection to mine, and to grant to the prayers of this soul, who loves Thee with so much fervour, all she asks of Thee." Then the Saint addressed our Lord thus: "O sweetness of my soul! O Jesus, most loving and most desirable! O dearest of all who are dear!" After having said these and many similar words, she exclaimed: "What fruit can there be in these words, uttered by one so vile?" Our Lord replied: "What does it matter what kind of wood is used to stir up perfumes and vases of incense, since, whatever they are stirred with, they always emit the same odour? Thus, when any one says to Me, 'My sweetest Lord,' &c., what does it matter if they think themselves utterly vile, since My goodness, like a perfume stirred up, exhales an odour in which I take extreme pleasure, and which gives to those who move it by their words a sweetness which is to them a foretaste of eternal life?"

CHAPTER V.

VISION OF OUR BLESSED LADY ON CHRISTMAS
NIGHT.

N the night of the Nativity, at Matins, as the Saint continued these exercises, our Lord, to correspond with her movements of fidelity and devotion, drew her entirely to Himself, so that, by a sweet influence of His Divinity in her soul, and by a reflux of knowledge which passed from her soul to God, she knew all that was chanted at Matins, whether Responsories or Psalms; and this knowledge gave her ineffable and incomprehensible joy. While this continued, she beheld all the saints standing before the throne of the King of kings, reciting Matins with great devotion, for His Divine honour and glory.

Remembering several persons who had been recommended to her prayers, she said, with great humility: "How can I, who am so unworthy, pray for persons who stand praising Thee with such labour and devotion, since my infirmity prevents me from following their example?" Our Lord replied: "You can very well pray for these persons, for I have hidden you in the bosom of My paternal goodness, that you may ask and obtain from Me whatever you will." "But, Lord," replied the Saint, "since it pleases Thee that I should pray for them, I beseech Thee to appoint a time in which I may do so with fidelity, in a manner worthy of Thee, and with utility to them, without losing the happiness with which Thou dost honour me in partaking of Thy celestial joys." To this our Lord replied : "Recommend each to My Divine kindness and love, since it is this love that has made Me descend from the bosom of My Father to serve men." When she had named each individually, our Lord, won by His tender love, supplied the needs of each by a most loving compassion.

After this, the Blessed Virgin appeared to her, seated honourably near her Divine Son ; and while the *Descendit de cœlis** was chanted,

---

* The Responsory, iv. Lesson, i. Nocturn, Matins for Christmas : "Descendit de cœlis Deus verus, a Patre genitus, introivit in uterum Virginis, nobis ut appareret visibilis, indutus carne humana protoparente edita : Et exivit per clausam portam, Deus et homo, lux et vita, conditor munda."—"The true God, born of the Father, descended from heaven, and entered into the Virgin's womb, that He might appear visibly to us, clothed with the flesh given to our first parents, and came forth our Lord appeared to recall the extreme goodness which had made Him descend from the bosom of His Father into that of the Virgin, and He looked so lovingly upon His Mother, as to move her very heart; and by His embrace He renewed all the joys which she had when in the world in His holy Humanity.

She also beheld the sacred and virginal womb of the Mother of God, which was clear as crystal, and in which our Lord appeared in the form of an infant, and flew promptly and lovingly to her heart : by this she understood that as the Humanity of Christ fed upon her virginal milk, .so did His Divinity feed on the purity and love of her heart. At the Response *Verbum caro factum est*,* when all the sisters made a profound

---

through the closed gate God and Man, Light and Life, the Maker of the world." This *clausam portam* of Ezechiel is constantly referred by the Fathers to the Blessed Virgin. St. Bernard, in his sermon on the Twelve Privileges B.V.M., says Mary is the eastern gate which none could pass but one. St. Jerome writes: "She (Mary) is the eastern gate of which Ezechiel speaks as always closed." St. Augustine, in his sermon on the Nativity : "The closed gate is the emblem of the integrity of her immaculate flesh. She remained inviolate after childbirth, and became more holy by conception."

* Responsory. xii. Lesson, iii. Nocturn ; the *Te Deum* follows, and on Christmas night the Midnight Mass is said, after which Lauds are commenced.

inclination to honour the Incarnation of Jesus Christ, she heard Him saying : " Whenever any one inclines at these words, from gratitude and devotion, giving Me thanks for having become Man for his sake, I also incline to him, by a pure movement of My goodness; and I offer, from My inmost Heart, all the fruit and merit of My Humanity to God the Father, that the eternal beatitude of this person may be doubled."

At the words *et veritatis*, the Blessed Virgin came forth, with the double ornament of her virginity and her maternity, and, accosting the first sister on the right side of the choir, she embraced her closely, presenting her Divine Son, whom she held in her arms ; and in this manner she proceeded to each sister, allowing each to embrace this incomparably amiable Child. Amongst those who were thus favoured, some held Him in their arms most carefully, appearing very anxious that He should suffer no inconvenience ; others, on the contrary, neglected these precautions, and permitted His Head to hang down in a very painful manner. By this she understood, that those who had no will but that of God, rested the Head of the loving Jesus on a soft pillow, that supported

Him, by their good will; while those whose
wills were inflexible and imperfect allowed the
Head of the Infant Jesus to hang down incon-
veniently.   Therefore, my beloved, let us empty
our hearts and consciences of all self-will, and
offer our hearts to our Lord with full and entire
obedience to His good pleasure, since He only
seeks our spiritual advancement.   Why should
we disturb, even by the merest trifle, the repose
and consolation of so delicate and tender an Infant, who comes to us with such goodness and
love !

At the Mass *Dominus dixit*,* our Lord again
imparted to her a knowledge of all that was
said, which gave her ineffable joy.

Then, from the *Gloria in excelsis* to the words
Primogenitus Mariæ virginis matris, she began to
think that the title of only Son was more
suitable than that of the first-born, because the
Immaculate had only brought forth this Son,
whom she merited to conceive by the power of
the Holy Ghost ; but the Blessed Virgin said to
her sweetly : " Call my beloved Jesus my first-
born, rather than my only begotten, for I

* The Introit of the first or Midnight Mass.   *Primogenitus*—probably a reference to the Gospel for that
Mass.

brought Him forth first; but after Him, or
rather by Him, I have made you His brethren
and my children, when I adopted you as such
by the maternal affection which I have for
you."

At the Offertory, the Saint, in spirit, beheld
the sisters offering to our Lord all the devotions
which they had performed during Advent.
Some placed them in the bosom of the Divine
Infant, whose image had been impressed on
their souls; and the Blessed Virgin inclined
towards each with unparalleled condescension,
placing her Divine Son so that He could receive
in His Hands what they offered; others appeared
to advance towards the altar, and remained
in the centre of the choir, where they offered
their prayers to the Blessed Virgin and to her
Son; but He was not placed so that He could
receive them, and made signs to that effect.
She understood from this, that those who placed
their offerings in the bosom of the Child Jesus,
were they who were united to the Lord with
their whole hearts, wherein He was spiritually
born, and that the Blessed Virgin assisted them
in this with all her power, rejoicing with them
in their devotion and spiritual advancement;
but those persons who had offered their gifts in

the centre of the choir were they who only thought of the Birth of our Lord on the Festival, and because they were reminded of it by the special devotion of the Church.

Then this blessed soul approached the King of Glory, to present Him the good-will of those who would have accomplished many things, had they not been hindered by a lawful cause. And she was instructed in spirit that all the prayers which had been made with devotion were placed as pearls in the tablet, and that the good-will of those who would have performed the same devotions, had they not been occupied, and who grieved and consequently humbled themselves for this omission, should be placed in the chain with which our Lord's bosom was adorned, and that they would obtain such advantage from this nearness to the Heart of Jesus, that they would be as if they had the key of a treasure which contained all they could desire.

CHAPTER VI.

HOW WE SHOULD SALUTE AND HONOUR THE BLESSED MOTHER OF GOD.

AS St. Gertrude was ill, on the solemnity of the Assumption, she was unable to fulfil her intention of saying as many *Ave Marias* as the Blessed Virgin had been years on earth ; but she tried to supply for this devotion in some degree by the three aspirations—*Ave Maria, gratia plena, Dominus tecum.* As she offered them with great fervour for herself and those committed to her care, our Lady appeared to her in glory, clothed with a green mantle covered with golden flowers in the form of trefoils, and said to her : " Behold how I am adorned with as many flowers as those for whom you have prayed have uttered words in their petition to me ; the brilliancy of these flowers corresponds to the fervour of their petitions; and I will turn this to their advantage, to render them more agreeable to my Son and all the celestial court."

St. Gertrude observed also that the Blessed Virgin had some roses with six leaves amongst the trefoils, and that three of these leaves were golden, and enriched with precious stones; while the other three, which alternated with the former, were distinguished by an admirable variety of colours. The three golden leaves indicated the threefold divisions of the *Ave Maria* which she had made during her sickness; and the three other leaves were added by our Lord—the first to reward her for the love with which she saluted and praised His most sweet Mother; the second, for her discretion and prudence in regulating her devotions during her illness; and the third, for the confidence which she had that the Lord and His loving Mother would accept the little she had done.

At *Prime*, St. Gertrude besought our Lord to obtain His Blessed Mother's favour for her, as she feared she had never been sufficiently devout to her. Our Lord then, after bestowing many marks of tenderness and filial affection on His Divine Mother, said to her: "Remember, My beloved Mother, that for your sake I am indulgent to sinners, and regard My elect as if she had served you all her life with devotion."

At these words this most pure Mother gave herself entirely to Gertrude, for the sake of her Divine Son. As the Collect *Deus, qui virgi-*

*nalem,** was read at Mass, our Lord appeared to renew in His Blessed Mother all the joys which she had experienced in His Conception, His Birth, and the other Mysteries of His Humanity. At the words *Ut sua nos defensione munitos,*† which the Saint read with special devotion, she beheld the Mother of God extending her mantle as if to receive beneath its shelter all those who fled to her patronage. The holy angels then brought all who had prepared themselves very fervently for this Feast, and presented them to her as fair young virgins, who stood before her as before their mother; while these good angels defended them from the snares of evil spirits, and carefully incited them to good actions.

The Saint understood that they had obtained this angelic protection by the words *Ut sua defensione,* &c.; for at her command the angels never fail to protect and defend those who invoke this glorious Virgin.

* Collect for the Mass of the Assumption.
† "That defended by her protection," &c.

CHAPTER VII.

HOW THE MOTHER OF GOD ASSISTS SINNERS.

NUMBER of little animals* appeared afterwards under the mantle of the Blessed Virgin; and this signified those sinners who addressed themselves to her with devotion. The Mother of Mercy received them with the greatest charity, and covered them with her mantle; thus manifesting with what affability she treats those who have recourse to her; how she protects them even during their wanderings; and if they recognize their faults, and return to her, she reconciles them to her Son by a sincere penance. At the Elevation, St. Gertrude saw our Divine Lord imparting Himself, with all the joys of His Divinity and Humanity, to all those who had assisted at Mass with special devotion in honour of His Blessed Mother, and who had desired to serve. her devoutly on the day of her Assumption; so that, being sustained by virtue of the adorable Sacrament, they were strengthened

* " Diversi generis bestiolæ."

in their good desires, even as food strengthens and invigorates the human frame.

After Mass the community proceeded to Chapter, and the Saint saw a multitude of angels surrounding our Lord, who appeared to wait with great joy for the arrival of the religious. Marvelling at this, she said to our Lord : " Why has Thou come to this Chapter, O most loving Lord, surrounded by such a multitude of angels, since we have not the same devotion now as on the Vigil of Thy Divine Birth ?" Our Lord replied : " I come as the Father of a family, to receive those who have been invited to eat at My house. I come also from respect to My Mother, to announce the solemn Festival of her eminent Assumption, and to receive all who are prepared to celebrate this Feast with holy disposition. I come also to absolve, by the virtue and authority of My Divinity, all those who humble themselves for the negligences which they have committed concerning their Rule." He added : " I am present on all these Festivals, and see all that you do, although, on the Vigil of My Nativity, I assisted in an extraordinary manner."

CHAPTER VIII.

HOW ST. GERTRUDE RECITED NONE AND VESPERS IN HONOUR OF THE BLESSED VIRGIN.

AS St. Gertrude recited None with special devotion, it was revealed to her that on the day previous to the Assumption of the Blessed Virgin she had been so absorbed in God, from the hour of None until the moment of her happy departure from this world, as to have nothing human in her, to live only by the Spirit of God, and to taste in anticipation all those celestial joys which she soon experienced perfectly and eternally in the bosom of God; and that at the third hour of the night our Lord came for and took her to Himself with exceeding joy.

In the evening, at Vespers, the Saint beheld our Lord drawing into His Heart all the praises which had been chanted in honour of His Blessed Mother, and from thence pouring them forth upon her in an impetuous torrent. As the Antiphon *Ista pulchra es* was chanted, St. Gertrude offered the words to our Lord through

His Sacred Heart, in memory of the sweet caresses He had bestowed on His Blessed Mother by the same words; and this devotion, passing through the Heart of Jesus to the heart of Mary, encircled her like a cincture of stars, consoling her in a marvellous manner. Many of these stars appeared to fall to the ground;* but the saints gathered them up, presenting them to our Lord with joy and admiration. This signified that all the saints obtain ineffable joy, glory, and beatitude from the superabundant merits of the Blessed Virgin.

When the community chanted the Response *Quæ est ista?*† the angels united with them in singing it. Our Lord Himself intoned the *Ista est speciosa*, the Holy Spirit animating His Divine Heart to praise and glorify the most excellent of all creatures.

At the hymn *Quem terra, pontus*, the Blessed Virgin seemed unable to contain the plenitude of her delights, and reclined on the bosom of her Son until the words *O gloriosa Domina*.‡

---

* "Pavimentum."

† iv. Ant. at Vespers, but worded differently now. The other responses are also in the present Office, and the hymn *Quem terra*, &c.

‡ "O Queen of all the virgin choir;" Hymn at Lauds.

Then she appeared as if aroused by the devotion of the faithful, and extended her hands over them to protect and console them by her maternal love. At the verse *Deo Patri*, she rose again, and made three profound genuflexions, in honour of the Ever-blessed Trinity; and then she continued praying for the whole Church until the *Magnificat*. At the Antiphon *Virgo prudentissima*, she sent celestial light to all who invoked her devoutly.

On another occasion, at the Assumption, when St. Gertrude was so feeble as to be unable to assist at Matins, the Lord, the Orient from on high, visited her with ineffable goodness. It appeared to her at the sixth Response that she assisted in spirit at the moment when the Blessed Virgin paid the last debt of nature, and entered heaven. Her rapture continued from this response until the *Te Deum*, when she returned to herself once more; but during this rapture, she was favoured with a heavenly intelligence of all that was chanted, which filled her with ineffable joy.

CHAPTER IX.

HOW ST. GERTRUDE WAS CONSOLED IN HER SICKNESS.

THREE years after the occurrence of the favours just related, the Saint was confined to bed on the Vigil of the Assumption; nevertheless she endeavoured to prepare herself for this great festival with all possible fervour and devotion. While she was thus occupied, she beheld the Blessed Virgin in a beautiful garden, cultivated with the greatest care, and filled with rare flowers. Our Lady appeared to be in a rapture caused by an excess of repose and joy, the serenity of her countenance and her gestures indicating that she was full of grace. In this garden there were roses without thorns, lilies white as snow, and fragrant violets, with many other flowers. But it seemed very marvellous that the farther these flowers were from the Blessed Virgin, the brighter was their colour and the sweeter their fragrance. Then she appeared to draw this odour to herself by inspiration, and to pour it forth into the Heart of her Son, which seemed to be opened for this purpose. A great number of angels were also in this garden, between these flowers and the Blessed Virgin, who served God by proclaiming her praises. St. John the Evangelist also remained near her, praying fervently, and she appeared to attract his prayers to herself like a sweet vapour.

As St. Gertrude took singular pleasure in this vision, she began to marvel what it might mean; and our Lord taught her that the garden signified the chaste body of the Blessed Virgin; that the flowers were her virtues; that the beautiful roses which appeared so far from her were the actions which she had performed for the love of God and her neighbour, and which increased in merit as the love which prompted them was extended; that the lilies signified her extreme purity; and that the prayers of St. John, which she appeared to attract, signified the glory which she had received through him, in consequence of the care which he had taken of her while on earth, that she might be enabled to spend more time in prayer.

Then she inquired what advantage St. John had gained from this; and our Lord replied: "My Heart was drawn more towards him for ⁻⁻⁻h act of devotion which he offered to My

Mother." Lastly, she understood that the vision of the Blessed Virgin which she had seen represented her soul, which always abounded in the fruits of virtue, and which she ever returned to God with the greatest thanksgiving.

At Matins, she was again rapt in ecstasy, and beheld the Blessed Virgin reposing sweetly and peaceably upon her Divine Son, and the Son pouring forth into the heart of His Mother an ineffable joy, the fruit of the virtues which she had practised, and had returned to Him as their true and only Source. The Eternal Father seemed to chant the first Responsory, *Vidi speciosam*,* by which the whole celestial court understood that the Blessed Virgin had indeed been a dove in purity and innocence ; that she ascended above the rivers of waters by desire ; that her garment—that is, her holy life—was full of ineffable sweetness; and that she was surrounded with roses and lilies—that is, with every virtue.

* *Vidi speciosam*, i. Response, i. Nocturn, Feast of the Assumption : " I have seen thee, beautiful as a dove, ascending above the rivers of waters ; the odour of thy garment was ineffable, and thou wert encompassed with roses and lilies. Who is this that cometh up from the desert like a cloud, perfumed with myrrh and incense ?"

Then the Holy Ghost made known the holy life of the Blessed Virgin by chanting the Response *Sicut cedrus;* the saints, full of admiration and joy, adding the third Response, *Quæ est ista?* of which St. Gertrude received a marvellous understanding; but her infirmity caused her to forget it. The saints then passed in procession round the throne of the Blessed Virgin, chanting the fourth Response, *Gaude regina,* with profound respect and with a marvellous concord of voices, praising this mighty Queen on whom the eternal light shone so gloriously; so that she appeared to all in heaven and earth as the most beautiful and accomplished Virgin in virtue and grace—as a Mother who provides for our wants, and who will increase our glory and crown our joy and beatitude hereafter.

Deo Gratias.

LITTLE OFFICE OF ST. GERTRUDE.

MATINS.

V. O Lord, open Thou my lips.
R. And my mouth shall declare Thy praise.
V. Incline unto my aid, O God.
R. O Lord, make haste to help me.
Glory be to the Father, &c.

HYMN.

Dilecte Sponse.

Dear Spouse of Virgins, hear us sing
  With joy a virgin's praise,
Whom Thou didst in Thy love prepare
  To join angelic lays.

And hear us, too, O Gertrude, now,
  While we thy joys proclaim,
Chanting this office with sweet voice,
  In honour of thy name.

Praise be to Father, and to Son,
  And to the Paraclete,
By whom this spouse unto her Lord
  Was joined in union sweet.

PRAYER.

Deus qui. O God, who didst delight to dwell in the most pure heart of the blessed Gertrude, purify our hearts by her merits and intercession, that they may become a habitation worthy of Thy Divine Majesty: who liveth and reigneth with Thee, in the unity of the Holy Ghost, world without end. Amen.

LAUDS.

V. Incline, &c.

HYMN.

Before all ages thou wert chosen,
  O Gertrude, to obtain
The richest treasures which the love
  Of Christ thy Spouse can gain.

For this be praise to God on high,
  And unto Christ thy love,
With holy and eternal laud
  To the co-equal Dove.

PRAYER.—*Deus qui.* O God, &c.

PRIME.

V. Incline, &c.

HYMN.

Thy early dawn of life was filled
  With equal love and light,
Which sweetly drew thy heart and soul
  To realms of pure delight.
          For this, &c.
PRAYER.—*Deus qui.* O God, &c.

TIERCE.

V. Incline, &c.

HYMN.

Thou hast no other spouse but Christ,
　　To Him thy pure soul turns;
And every thought of other love
　　For love of Him is spurned.
　　　　　　　　　　For this, &c.

PRAYER.—*Deus qui.*　O God, &c.

SEXT.

V. Incline, &c.

HYMN.

Thy Spouse, within thy heart enthroned,
　　Keeps regal state, and finds His rest;
While others scorn His gentle rule,
　　Or drive away the heavenly Guest.
　　　　　　　　　　For this, &c.

PRAYER.—*Deus qui.*　O God, &c.

NONE.

V. Incline, &c.

HYMN.

Stronger than death is that strong love
　　Which burns within thy virgin breast,
Mourning thy Jesus slain for thee,
　　In whom alone thy heart can rest.
　　　　　　　　　　For this, &c.

PRAYER.—*Deus qui.*　O God, &c.

VESPERS.

V. Incline, &c.

HYMN.

With the right Hand of love He wounds,
  With the right Hand He victory gains ;
For love's own victim, who with Him,
  In everlasting triumph reigns.
               For this, &c.

PRAYER.—*Deus qui.*   O God, &c.

COMPLINE.

V. Incline, &c.

HYMN.

And now thy earthly race is o'er,
  The conqueror's crown and palm is won,
And thou wilt rest for evermore
  Upon the Heart of God's dear Son.
               For this, &c.

PRAYER.—*Deus qui.*   O God, &c.

Ora pro nobis beata Gertrudis : ut digne efficiamur
promissionibus Christi.

Made in the USA
Lexington, KY
17 November 2015